Beyond the Green Fields

The final memories of some of the first men of the Tank Corps

Compiled by
Richard Pullen MA

About the Author

Richard Pullen has been a field archaeologist for over a decade and although his particular interest is industrial archaeology, during his archaeological career he has directed sites of all periods throughout the British Isles. He gained a Masters Degree in Archaeology and Museum Management in 2004.

He has been writing professionally for over five years. His first book, 'The Landships of Lincoln' was published in 2003. It has recently been completely revised, with the second edition being released in 2007.

First Published in Great Britain in 2008 by Tucann Books
Text & Images © Richard Pullen
All rights reserved
Design © TUCANN*design&print*

ISBN 978-1-873257-92-0

Produced by: TUCANN*design&print*, 19 High Street, Heighington Lincoln LN4 1RG
Tel & Fax: 01522 790009 • www.tucann.co.uk

Also by the same author

The Landships of Lincoln-Second Edition
The story of Lincolns part in the invention of the first Tanks 1915-1918

Tanks of the Great War Colouring Book
An introduction into the world of Great War Tanks for the younger reader

Acknowledgements

With thanks to Ray Hooley, ex-secretary of the Lincoln Tank Group, for kindly lending me the precious tapes and photographs and for giving permission for them to be published. Due to the foresight of Ray and the rest of the group, an irreplaceable part of our history was recorded before it was lost forever.

The photographs of William Francis and the German DFW Aeroplane he shot down in 1917 were kindly loaned by Philippe Gorczynski, Great War Tank historian and author of 'Following the Tanks-Cambrai'

Thanks as always for the endlessly knowledgeable and cheerful assistance given by the Tank Museum at Bovington and especially David Fletcher.

A great deal of valuable information regarding the early days of the Motor Machine Gun Corps was located by the library staff of the Vintage Motor Cycle Club Ltd.

Thanks to Robin Wheeldon for kindly allowing me to use his 2005 painting 'WWI British Tanks in Action' as the front cover illustration for this book.

I am also grateful for the work undertaken by Alwyn Killingsworth and Joanne Pullen who tracked down many of the service histories of the soldiers mentioned in this book.

Just as vital in the production of this book were Grace and Avro who helped and encouraged me in their own special way.

Dedication

This book is dedicated to the memory of the brave men who went to war in the first Tanks, but particularly to the few surviving Tank Corps veterans who shared their stories and left them with us.

Harry Emans
Val Field
William Francis
Jack Moss
Ernest Sneath
Ted Waddington

A 1917 Pencil sketch drawn by an unknown artist of an unknown soldier of the Heavy Battalion Machine Gun Corps

Introduction

The horrific fighting of the Great War lasted from August 1914 until November 1918 and cost the lives of countless millions. It was a new way of fighting, for the first time in history it involved everyone, not just the military. It was Total War on a global scale and it changed the social, political and economic map of the world forever. The causes of this inevitable new global war were many and varied, but it was so appalling and bloody for just one reason, mechanization.

The industrialized countries of the world had been itching for an opportunity to do more than just rattle their sabres; they needed to try them out for real. They wanted to test their weaponry on a wide scale and in turn, develop new more efficient killing technology as a result. When war was declared in 1914, they got the chance they'd been waiting for, but once the cork was out of the bottle it could not easily be put back in again. The old rules of war were soon cast aside, with hellish, underhand devices such as flamethrowers and poison gas beginning to appear on the battlefield. Poison gas was arguably the most terrible and indiscriminate weapon developed up to that time and was the worst nightmare of every man fighting at the front. It had been invented by the Germans, but once unleashed; the Allies soon saw the potential of this new horror. The British and French armies had no compunction about using it and were not slow to catch up and even overtake in the race for the next even more lethal gas. The war was supposed to be over by Christmas 1914, but this was not just over optimistic, it was ridiculous. It was nothing short of a lie perpetuated by the politicians and the military in order to keep up morale and encourage enlistment. The arms race snowballed and became unstoppable. In a vain attempt to protect themselves the two opposing armies had been forced to dig defensive trenches. Soon, these trenches became longer, wider and more elaborate until miles of the western front was scarred with a warren of subterranean barracks. Once and army had dug in, its mobility was effectively lost; without an advance and the taking of enemy ground and positions the war could not be won by either side. The magnificent rush for glory of the summer of 1914 had now become a festering dead end. The war to end all wars had stagnated and would never move again until the trenches were broken, the politicians came to their senses or everyone was dead.

Time after time the attacks began with preliminary barrages, whistles blowing and men going over the top. Unfortunately, all too often the enemies wire entanglements would slow down the attack and then the machine guns would finish it off for good. Somehow, the wire and enemy guns would need to be overcome and only then could the trenches be broken, thus making it possible for the war to move again. This became know as 'The Riddle of the Trenches' This apparently unsolvable dilemma lead to one of the most exciting and pivotal arms races of all time. At last, after several failed prototypes and unworkable machines, on 15th September 1916 the mythical, trench busting weapon made its debut for the Allies at Flers on the western front. The new machines were known variously as Landships, Machine gun Destroyers, Armoured Toads, Trench Dreadnaughts, Big Willies, Ospreys, Buses or Snarks. Finally they became officially designated as 'Tanks' and this simple ambiguous title would become feared throughout the world. At last the Tank had been created and surely now the war would be over in a matter of days?

Unfortunately, due mainly to the unprecedented urgency attached to the creation of this new weapon, the Tank was a rush job and had been constructed mainly from 'off the peg' parts and materials. William Foster and Co Ltd of Lincoln had created the first machines by using little more than flat boiler-plate and parts from agricultural vehicles already in their range and although it was a well engineered and very capable piece of forward thinking technology it was not quite the war winner that everyone had been hoping for. The desperate need for the Tank was too far ahead of the technology available to physically build it. As if this wasn't bad enough, perhaps an even bigger problem was that the first Tanks were a completely new creation, untested, like nothing ever made before and with no precedent as to how to use them in battle. Special tactics for Tank warfare and crew training were months away and the people who planned the battles and directed the Tanks had no idea what they could and couldn't do. The military 'Top Brass' had been told that a Tank was impervious to just about any calibre of gun fire and that, thanks to its tracks, it could cross any type of terrain, regardless of shell holes, wire, trenches or flooding. Despite heroic efforts from the Tanks and their crews, the Generals would soon realize that most of the initial hype was far from true. The first Tanks needed constant maintenance, were underpowered, heavy, slow and difficult to control. They were ideally suited to large scale anti-personnel work on flat, unbroken ground. The first attacks using a handful of Tanks on the desolate and sodden battlefields at Flers and Ypres were near disasters and almost brought about the end for the new invention before it had even had a chance to fight. There were calls from many in Government and in the military to end the madness and scrap the Tanks before any more lives and money was wasted. Despite this, the Tank crews still had faith in their machines and knew that if they could only get the chance to prove their worth away from the quagmires of Belgium they could change everyone's minds and perhaps even change the course of the war.

The Tanks and their crews finally got the chance they had been waiting for on the 20th November 1917 when they assembled on mass for the now legendary Battle of Cambrai. A total of 476 Tanks were fielded for the first day of the battle and along with their supporting infantry they pushed the enemy further than anyone could ever have dreamed and back in England church bells were rung in celebration of the great victory of the Tanks. Regrettably the Battle of Cambrai was not the victory it had first appeared to be. At the end of the first day, 179 out of the original 476 machines had been lost, due to enemy fire, break downs or being ditched on unsuitable ground. The Tanks gains were not properly exploited by the supporting infantry and cavalry, a Tank is perfect for taking enemy positions, but is not very good for holding them. When the inevitable German counter-attack came, they pushed the British right back again, almost back to where they had started from on the first day. This has been blamed on a number of factors such as poor leadership at General Headquarters or the fact that the cavalry failed to turn up as arranged. It is just as likely that the failure to exploit the gains was purely because nobody had expected the Tanks to advance as far as they did. Whatever the reason, the battle finally ended as a virtual draw in men lost and ground taken, but it had shown what could be achieved by a disciplined crew in the latest Mark IV on good ground. Now that the Generals were clear on just what a Tank could really do, their place in the British Army was never in question again. Due mainly to overoptimistic reports in the press, back on the Home Front the British public was completely unaware of the tactical shortcomings of The Battle of Cambrai. They feverishly embraced the Tank as their saviour, the industrial and scientific solution to the new technological war that they had been expecting since 1914. The men of the Tank Corps had always believed vehemently in the new weapon and knew that it could change the Allies fortunes if only it was given the chance it deserved, Cambrai was that chance and they had seized it with both hands. The Tanks played a pivotal part in many battles of the Great War and although badly mauled in the German push of March 1918, they fought back and helped secure final victory when the British pushed back at Amiens. The Allies 'Big Push' began on the 8th August 1918 and was famously described by the German General Ludendorff as 'the blackest day of the German army'.

There are many books that cover the invention, testing and use of the first Tanks and this introduction is intended to give only the very briefest taste of the Tanks first tentative steps onto the battlefield from 1916 to 1918. Not usually so thoroughly recorded by the history books are the stories of the men who had to crew these early machines. The first Tanks broke down on a regular basis, were underpowered, poorly armoured and offered little or no protection to anything larger than small arms fire. Tank Corps losses were ridiculously high, running at a remarkable 40%. Even if the enemy guns didn't get you there was a very good chance that you would be asphyxiated by poisonous carbon monoxide fumes from your own Tanks leaking exhaust system. Many of the top brass from your own army thought you were useless and wanted to disband your corps and if you did manage to avoid the axe, the work was hard, the fighting was bloody and the rewards were few. What sort of a man would want to join the Tank Corps, where you were the main target for every enemy gunner for miles around? Perhaps they were patriotic, medal seeking adventurers? Maybe they were thugs or criminals who had changed their names and were trying to escape from their original regiments before the Military Police caught up with them? Perhaps they were simply young men who wanted to do their bit for King and Country and were good with engines? The truth is that the first men in the Tank Corps were all of these things and more besides. Various diaries and memoirs have been published over the years by the men who were there, they saw the war as it truly was and wrote down what they saw, perhaps hoping future generations would learn from them and not repeat the same mistakes. These men were usually officers and they told of commanding the Tanks, winning Military Crosses and the terrible sights they'd seen, but for every man who secured publisher and told his story there were a hundred who quietly returned to their old lives and never said a word about their years as a 'Tanky'.

At the time of writing there are only a few Great War survivors left in the world and all too soon they will also leave us and the turbulent times they lived through will pass out of living memory and become history. The lucky ones who did survive often never made it to old age because of wounds or gas inhalation with many men dying from their injuries years after they had received them. For every man who died without telling his story, an irreplaceable part of his nations military and social heritage was lost forever. For this reason, in the mid 1980s The Lincoln Tank Group decided to find as many Tank Corps veterans as they possibly could and record their memories of the war. They were only just in time as even then, seventy years after the war, they managed to interview just six. Most of these men had never even spoken to their own families about their experiences in the war, but with perseverance and the occasional well-meaning subterfuge the stories eventually came out. For the first time they spoke of the everyday details of enlistment, training and battle and every word was recorded. Between them their stories covered the entire history of the use of the Tank in the Great War. From Officers to Gunners, Motor Machine Gun Corps to Tank Corps, from the first actions of 1916 to Amiens in 1918 their experiences told the entire tale of the Tanks, first hand. The basic chronology of the Tank Corps experiences in war was roughly the same in each of the men's stories, but their individual experiences and their reactions to what was going on around them were all unique. Now, over 20 years after the recordings were made, these men have all passed away and without the invaluable work undertaken by the Lincoln Tank Group their stories would have died along with them. Even the group itself no longer exists, but thanks to industrial historian and the custodian of the tapes, Ray Hooley, the good work of the group has been preserved and the Tank Corps veterans recorded interviews have been saved. The crackly old reel-to-reel tape recordings have now been dusted off, transcribed and the following book is a text of those original recordings. The interviewers questions have been removed, the stories have been reordered to run chronologically and any extra information has been added in brackets, but otherwise, their words are unchanged. Although these brave men are now all long gone, their enthralling and unique recorded memories still survive, giving us a fascinating archive and a window into the life of both the Tank Corps and the British Army of over 90 years ago.

The Tank Corps colours are red, brown and green. These colours apparently signify the tanks going through blood, through mud and to the green fields beyond. The following six men went through the mud and the blood and lived to go beyond the green fields.

200585 Sgt. Harry Emans

Aged 87 when interviewed

Motor Machine Gun Corps (Heavy Section) 1916-17
Tank Corps 'C' Battalion 1917-19

When I first joined up it wasn't the Tank Corps, it was the Motor Machine Gun Service, Tanks were not yet then in existence, but eventually this Motor Machine Gun Service became the basis for the Tanks which were still sort of in embryo. Eventually it did develop into being the Tank Corps, but that was a long time later. At this time we didn't know anything about Tanks, we didn't even know they existed and all sorts of rumours began to float through the group. We were trained to use the Vickers machine gun and the 6 pounder gun and still we had no idea what we were destined for. A vague rumour began to float around suggesting that there was some sort of new armoured car and we went down to Whale Island near Portsmouth and did a course on using the 6 pounder gun at sea and how to strip it and reassemble it and all that sort of thing and yet we still had no idea what it was all about. A little later some of us were sent to a place called Thetford in Norfolk where there was a secret area where everybody, the farmers and so on, had been cleared out of. So

*Harry Emans, standing fourth from the right, and other fresh-faced recruits at Bisley Camp in 1916
(Ray Hooley)*

13

many square miles of it had had big shell holes dug and trenches dug and this was the first time we ever saw a Tank, we'd had no idea about it at all.

After we'd been there a week or so we were taken out for a ride in a Tank, but we still didn't know how they were to be used or anything. Quite suddenly one day we were given orders to move and were sent out to France, the Somme, this was September 1916.

We'd had no actual practical training along with the infantry or anything like that at all and we had to learn as we went along. We had this attack, I forget the date, but unfortunately the Tank I was allotted to developed engine trouble and we didn't even get past the starting point, so we didn't see the first part of the battle. From then on we hadn't got a Tank at all, so I was used to carry ammunition, guard ammunition dumps and so on. As the battle progressed the Tanks gradually dropped out and we had a go at trying to get one or two back to our lines, but the shell holes were so big and the ground was so terrible that it was quite a job and of course, the battle gradually petered out. By the middle of November the battle was practically over and we were brought back and put under canvas in a camp three or four miles back. While we were trying to get the Tanks into action it was the middle of November and just on the edge of the fighting was a place called Beaumont Hamel and hanging on the barbed wire were the bodies of the men who'd been killed on the wire in July, the bodies were still there and their uniforms were hanging there blowing in the breeze. Nearby, only a few hundred yards away on the parapet of the German front line were the bodies of British and Germans who'd fought it out with a bayonet, a terrible sight and I've never forgotten it after all these years, I was very young.

Anyway, as I say we were brought back and we had two days trip by train, forty men to a truck, and two days on the way, quite an experience. We detrained at a little place called Anvin and we still didn't know what was happening. We paraded outside on the forecourt of the station and divided into three groups and we then realized that we were all going to be spit up, these three groups were going to form the basis of the new battalion, three companies to a battalion which would be C Battalion instead of C Company. I was a bit worried in a way as my pal Freddie Smith was deputized to a different group to me, but we stopped half way to the next village and when we fell in again I fell in with his company and some-how this was never spotted. I was with him until he was killed at Arras a bit later *(206140 Private (Signaller) Frederick Smith Heavy Battalion Machine Gun Corps. Killed in action 11th April 1917).* Anyway we were

May 1917, from left to right standing, Gnr. Fergusson, Gnr. Harry Emans, Gnr. Edger Waddington, Gnr. Fred Smith. Front row seated Sgt. Charles Parrott, Lt. Thomson, Gnr. H.J. Wienche. Only seven members of the eight man crew are present as Gnr. Rawson was wounded at Arras in April 1917 (Ray Hooley)

going to a place called Erin, a tiny little scruffy village where we were bil-leted in old barns and stables, it was a quite interesting village really. The cold was intense and we had cavalry mess tins which were flat, not like the ordinary ones and if you didn't drink your tea fairly quickly it used to freeze. It was very cold, we had just two blankets on the wire netting beds and the coal trains from the north used to run through this village, a single line and there was a loop there where they had to stop. It wasn't long before the British soldier, being what he is, found this out and we used to scramble on and throw the coal down onto the railway line and pick it up later. The French guard used to run up and down blowing his little trumpet, but we didn't mind, we had to keep warm. We used a big five gallon oil drum and put a little grease drum inside it and put clay all round it and then got some pieces of iron that we scrounged and made really good stoves.

The winter was quite bad, but out of the blue it was rather relieved by a trip to the French Tank school not far from Fontainebleau. We took two Tanks down there and demonstrated them in front of what seemed to me to be the staff of all the armies, there were hundreds of staff officers watching this and trying to decide what type of Tank the British would adopt. We had a ride in the French Tanks which we didn't consider to be much good, to be truthful.

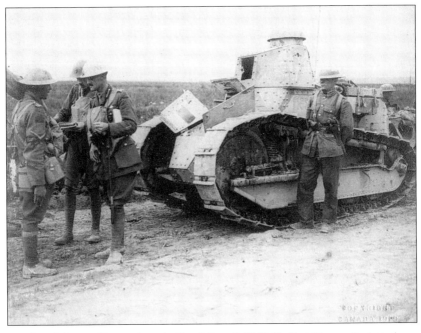

British Tank Corps soldiers evaluate the French Renault FT-17 (The Tank Museum, Bovington)

We had a quite interesting time there, we stayed for about a fortnight and we had a French cook and the food was quite good, it was a fascinating experience. We were there for Christmas and we had our Christmas dinner there. The officers were supposed to treat us, there were only three officers, two crew officers and a mechanical officer and the two Tank crews. When we took the two Tanks back, when it was time to leave, normally we would drive up a ramp and straight onto the train, but when we came to this station there was no ramp and we had to try to load the Tanks straight off the station platform. It was only a very small station and it was getting dark and every time we got the Tank crossways and then tried to swing it straight, we'd fetch the blasted truck off the line. Believe it or not we did it time and time again and every time we'd fetch the truck off the line, we were all fed up to the back teeth. It was raining and of course it was cold and right in the middle of it a Gendarme came down with the proprietor of the café where we'd had our evening meal and it seems that the officer had forgotten to pay the bill, so we had a whip around, I don't know how we did it, but we cleared it all up. Eventually we got the Tanks on and coming back took two days, it was very slow and at times we could walk beside the train. We had just one day's ration and soon we had very little left. We had tea and tinned milk and sugar and very little else. I begged some French bread from a troop train that had stopped at one of the stations and we scrounged some cider apples from a truck that had stopped at one of the places where we were. Well, our innards were a bit sore after this and we were very glad the next time we saw a tin of Bully Beef and some jam.

We did a bit more training, at the time we were very short of Tanks and we constructed a sort of Tank shaped canvas and wood frame about seven or eight feet long and four or five feet wide, with slits cut in the canvas and we would walk around the fields with this and pretend, so that we could get used to peering through the sides of the Tank, I don't know what the French farmers thought about it all, it must have looked a bit funny. Then we started training on a new gun, the Lewis Gun. We used to do this in the kitchen of the local shoemaker who'd been at Verdun and lost one eye, he was quite a character. We would practice how to strip it, behind your back and blindfolded so that we knew how to deal with it. In my little part of the barn we had two chaps who were what we called the Sanitary Walla's, they were always known to everybody as Spit and Cough. They were great singers, both Geordies, one was small and cross eyed and the other one was still small but rather stout. One of their favourite songs was 'Come, come speak to me Thora' and they used to nearly cry over it. Another song that was a great favourite, as the average Tommy is very sentimental, was 'There's an old mill near the stream, Nelly dear'. Strangely enough in this village there was indeed a stream and there was actually a corn mill with a little wooden foot bridge across it. At nights, every now and again, four or five of us used to go and stand on this bridge and sing 'There's an old mill near the stream, Nelly dear'. We used to buy those big, round French loaves from the bakery.

An excellent replica Mk I Female tank gets some finishing touches. This tank could have been used for training or to confuse the Germans

Rumours began to circulate and we began to realize that we would soon be on the move. The next thing we knew we were on route with a train load of Tanks bound for Arras. At that time we didn't realize what was coming off of course, but eventually we arrived at Arras. The front line ran close to the edge of it and we got there after a bit of a struggle in crossing some marshy ground after we'd detrained. The gun sponsons had to be removed before we could travel by train, otherwise it made the Tank too wide, so we had to take these things off and put them onto separate trucks and then drag them onto the back of the train and it was a terrible job. It was a problem to get these things off, mostly done at night of course, putting the sponsons onto little bogies and dragging them from truck to truck at the back of the Tanks. Driving a Tank onto a train at night with only about four inches to spares on either side was quite a problem as they are not easy to manoeuvre. Anyway, we made it and we left the Tanks in a place called the Citadel which was like a big moat around a fortress and we were billeted in cellars underneath the barracks. During that time, a fortnight or so, we never had any bread; believe it or not, we only had biscuits, little biscuits like dog biscuits. We had marmalade and soon we were heartily fed to the back teeth with marmalade, we'd had it for about six weeks and really we were sick of it. Finally the time for the attack came; it was timed for Easter Monday, April 9th 1917. We were only allowed out at night in small parties as we were very close to the front line. As you walked down the streets of Arras in single file in the semi darkness just before dawn you could hear the barrage just starting. We had a cooked breakfast that morning, the first for about two or three weeks and I thought to myself, if we don't come back we shall at least of had a cooked breakfast. Anyway, we started off in the Tanks and as we got

Male Mk II tank 'Iron Duke' trundles through the ruins of Arras. The tank was still a relatively new invention and the infantry seem intrigued by its progress

near to the line I could see the infantry advancing with us and the battle was quite interesting as I was seeing it for the first time. Unfortunately we got to the German front line alright, but we ditched and we couldn't get out. We all got out with spades and what wood we could find and tried to dig it out, but it was pretty hopeless. The Germans were shelling quite heavily and suddenly I saw Gunner Lawson fall, he was one of our crew. I went over to him and he'd been wounded in the groin, I undid his trousers and saw that it wasn't really serious, but it was rather nasty. I put a field dressing on it and got a couple of captured Germans to carry

19

him on duck-boards down to the first aid station. Eventually we got going again, but by then the others had got a way ahead, so we just had to carry on. By then the attack had stopped and we stayed with our group until the next day. We spent the time in between greasing and oiling. The next day it snowed like blazes, it was a blizzard, but we stayed where we were. We were told that night that the next day we would be going on to attack a place called Monchy le Preux just a couple of miles further on, just off the Arras to Cambrai road. We were told that there would be no artillery barrage, which rather made our spirits droop. However, we started off again from this village. I was what we called secondary driver, responsible for changing secondary gears because you needed more than three men to drive them. I was also acting as a loader for the six pounder gunner as we were a man short as Gunner Lawson had been wounded on Easter Monday. My section officer, Captain May said he would come with us to take over so to speak. Anyway, we got near to this village and we could see all the guns going and we could see our own troops. I was kept very busy loading the gun for the 6 pounder gunner and also changing gear. Captain May had gone up to the front where the Tank commander was and I was at the Lewis Gun when I saw some Germans going down into a ditch. I fired a couple of drums off at them, but I hoped I'd only wounded them, strangely enough. We kept going and I kept loading for the 6 pounder gunner until we had what is called a misfire. A misfire is when the shell has been struck and not gone off, but it still could go off at any time. Anyway, I looked at him and he looked at me and I opened the sponson door and gently lowered the shell from the gun and dropped it outside. Shortly afterwards the engine stopped and we couldn't start it again, obviously we had a seized engine, so we just sat there. Captain May was absolutely fearless. He sat there calmly with a map across his knee. We were all on tenterhooks as we were in full view of the German Artillery and they kept getting near misses. To be quite truthful we were really scared as we expected to get hit at any minute. Captain May gave the order to abandon Tank and I grabbed the Lewis Gun and got out of the sponson door. By then we were in between the Germans and our own troops and we set off as best as we could and dropped into a trench held by our lads. We sat there for a while deciding what to do. Jerry was sweeping the parapet with machine gun fire, so we kept quite low. Eventually we decided that we'd better get going and we crawled along the trench and into a sunken ditch along the side of the road leading to Monchy le Preux. As we lay there we could see a small body of cavalry, maybe 20 or 30 of them I should think.

A Mk II male, number 799, abandoned on the battlefield after the battle of Bullecourt in 1917

They came galloping up the street and as they left the village they just seemed to melt until there were men and horses lying all over the road, it was a most terrible sight. Eventually we saw a Vickers machine gun team and we were going to follow them, but they were going to the front line so we decided that we'd better get back. As we were walking along I heard a man calling and I found and infantry Sergeant in a shell hole who had a bullet wound in the leg. I gave the Lewis Gun to one of my crew, Waddy, as I called him and got this man on piggyback and carried him along to a first aid station. We then saw a horse drawn GS ammunition wagon and we jumped onto it and managed to get back to Arras. That was the end of that episode.

The Germans would play a machine gun up and down the outside of a Tank and as far as they could see where there were little loopholes and what have you They didn't always pierce the loopholes, but they would splash lead pieces from the bullets and the little splashes would often come through and get into your eyes. This is why the crews would wear protective masks, but these obscured your vision so much that you couldn't always tell what you were supposed to be doing. You couldn't really see through them because if you had it low enough to stop the splashes you couldn't see what you were doing. What you used to do was try to shield your eyes with your hand and just put up with it. You couldn't hear yourself speak inside a Tank and when the first driver at the front

A chainmail mask and Machine Gun Corps soft cap as worn by tank crews in the Great War. Unsurprisingly, the masks were very unpopular with the crews

wanted a gear changing at the back he would bang on the engine cover and put two fingers up for second gear, one finger up for first gear and two fingers down if he wanted neutral. We had no method of communication with other Tanks. We were supposed to carry a man with semaphore flags, but obviously you couldn't put a man outside with flags as he would be shot at. There was an idea for using mechanical semaphore, but it was no good, you couldn't control it and there was no time to do it. There was an idea to have a telephone cable trailing out behind you, but the noise was so terrific that it would have been impossible for anyone to speak to you.

After the last battle we went back and started to make preparations, including drawing new Tanks and practice how to use them. They had been modified and the 6 pounders had been cut shorter, these were Mark IV Tanks. Instead of having to take the gun sponsons off, by now the factory had built it so that the flange that connected the gun sponson to the Tank was inside, so that all we had to do was to take out the bolts and push the sponson inwards sufficient to get clearance when passing other traffic. You couldn't do this with the long gun of course, so the 6 pounder was cut short and pushed back on its mountings which was a great improvement.

A brand new Female Mk IV at the Lord Mayors Show in London 1917

The next thing I remember was that I was sent out on an advance party, before a battle you've got to have established petrol, oil, ammunition, grease and everything that's necessary, everything that was needed. About 20 of us went to a place near Ypres, called Oosthoek Wood. We still didn't know what was on, but we knew we were coming onto something else. We were given about 20 West Africans who had been recruited to do what we called 'donkey work' and we started them off at one end of the wood with a load of 2 gallon petrol tins, four in a case. Then we would meet them at the other end to tell them where to dump it. We waited and half of them didn't turn up so we walked back through the wood and found them having a rest half way, we didn't really mind, I suppose it didn't really matter. Anyway, one night we were in bivouacs, I built myself a bivvy from corrugated iron and the Germans must have somehow got to know we were there as they began to shell the wood, not too heavily, but they did shell it and we had one or two casualties. The following night they started shelling again, but we brought this naval gun up by rail, it was a very big naval gun and a truck load of ammunition. They would bring it up at night, fire it at the Germans all night and then take it back away in the daytime. On one particular night, quite by accident I suppose, a German shell hit the ammunition truck and the resulting explosion was fantastic and there were pieces of railway lines, trucks, ammunition and what have you coming down, it really was the most awful explosion. Picking up the bits the next morning where chaps had been caught whilst trying to run for shelter was a bit of a grim business. Soon we moved on a bit and you always had to have a man in reserve and I was the reserve man used for carrying ammunition and so on up to the Tanks that were going over, until one man suddenly fell sick and I was detailed to take his place. I had left my revolver back at headquarters and I didn't like the idea of going over without one, so I mentioned this to my section officer and Captain May leant me his. We eventually got going over to where the battle was in progress and it was filth, you've never seen such terrible ground in your life. The last place the Tanks should have been sent to. The ground had been shelled for weeks and weeks and was one mass of shell holes and water. We kept on going and we got ditched several times, we managed to get going each time and we were creeping nearer and nearer until the front of one track was blown off. We got the order to abandon Tank and my pals and I started to scramble out, I grabbed the Lewis gun and got out. It really was the most awful place, you couldn't walk above a couple of yards without falling into a shell hole full of water and I be-

Usually only given to officers, but due to space restrictions every member of a tank crew was issued with a Mark VI .455 calibre Webley and Scott service revolver

Men, tanks and a precious opportunity wasted in the muddy morass of Flanders

lieve it was a fact that people who were wounded and fell into them could easily drown. As we plodded along I said to my pal 'Fancy sending Tanks into ground like this, whoever sent us here should have come and had a look at it first'. We kept on going and kept to the road, there was just one road and it was under German observation, you could see the German observation balloons. There were also some of those big pillboxes that the Germans had built on the side of the road, these were now being used as a hospital. You could see chaps lying on stretchers there and I thought how lucky we were that we could keep moving while they were just lying there. The people I admired were the infantry and the artillery who were out there in all that mud and water; they just had to stick it. When we came out of a Tank, we were still alive, alright we hadn't got a Tank anymore, but we were alive and we were finished until the next battle, but these poor blighters had got to stick it and stay there. They were the men I admired above all, more than anything. We did really curse the people back at Staff, who should have known that it was a waste of Tanks and men to send them into that sort of a battle. Gradually the Tanks got less and less because they were knocked out, when they were ditched and Germans shelled them, they were soon just useless. We went back and started to prepare for the next battle which was to be Cambrai. This was of course one of the really big battles of the war and I could talk about it all night. The Germans had built three lines of trenches, each one too wide for a Tank to bridge and we wondered how we could overcome this for a long time. They were protected by miles and miles of barbed wire, but it was decent ground and an area in which we could operate easily. It was all kept very secret, there was no firing, no artillery preparation at all and we moved only at night-time. The way they overcame the wide German trenches was by making fascines. They were huge bundles of brushwood carried on top of the Tanks. They were made by using two Tanks pulling with hawsers to draw them together. There was a lever inside the Tank so that you could loose them when needed. The idea was that the first wave of Tanks would go over the wire and onto the German front line where it would drop its fascine into the first trench. The next wave of Tanks would then come forward and cross over on the fascine and drop their fascines and so on until we got to the German trenches. Some of the Tanks were what we called wire cars as they carried a big anchor towed on a strong wire hawser. They crossed the barbed wire, which was no problem for the Tanks and pulled huge gaps in the wire with the anchors so that the infantry could walk over it. It is a fact that in twelve hours we

Female Mk IV 'Auld Reekie II' complete with its brushwood fascine (The Tank Museum, Bovington)

took as much ground as had taken three months at Passchendaele with an expenditure of I think around just 6000 casualties and as many Germans being taken prisoner. Cambrai was very successful, but at one little place called Flesquieres a German officer with an artillery group held up the attack for about half a day. I think he knocked out about six Tanks. I think they were F battalion, they should have not have been crossing one after another in the same place. Anyway the battle went well and we eventually managed to take Flesquieres, but by then Jerry had started to bring troops down from the north and was holding fast at a place called Bourlon Village and Bourlon Wood which was right on the edge of the salient that we'd formed. About six days later we were up in the salient and I was helping to relieve drivers who were coming out of the battle exhausted. I met them on the line and brought them back. I was in the village and suddenly a German aeroplane came over and we'd got about six observation balloons up and he went along the lot and shot them all down. Soon I began to think there must be something wrong as some artillery men started to come back carrying breech blocks and there were one or two transports who seemed to be in a great hurry. We were told that the Germans had broken through in the southern part of the salient and we were cut off, we would now have to fight our way out. Unfortunately at that time, we only had a skeleton crew, we'd sent the other four men back to the railhead as we were supposed to be withdrawn. We had only a four man crew so my officer sent me to get some maps from the dugout, but when I came out, the Tank had gone! It was all right in the end as we found that the German advance had been stopped by a Guards division that was moving out of the salient, but had turned back to fight the advance. It was quite exciting as a matter of fact.

Medium A Whippet number 217 'Julian's Baby' on test at Dollis Hill

Eventually, we became the third light battalion equipped with Whippet Tanks. It was a much smaller Tank, three crewmen only, a driver and two gunners. It had two engines, two gearboxes and was very tricky to drive. It was a little faster than the Mark IV, but used just the light machine gun. Ideal of course, once the bigger Tanks had broken the line they could put the Whippets in they could go much faster and try to exploit the attack. We were due for an attack at Saint Quentin, so we moved up a few miles. We parked up in a quarry that had been used by the Germans as a halting place and there were holes cut into the sides of the quarry. We stayed there the night, but the place was full of rats and at night you'd have your greatcoat over your head because the rats would be running all over. Soon I couldn't stand it any longer and got out and went and slept in the Tank, I was a bit stiff in the morning. We eventually got up to where the battle was in progress; I forget the name of the place. Well, I don't suppose I really should tell you the bit about the American Tank Corps, no I've leave that out.

Humieres in 1918. Harry Emans, now a sergeant, stands second from the left on the back row. On his left stands H. J. Wienche who was in the same crew as Harry in April 1917. Wienche is also now a sergeant. He would also survive the war and be awarded the Military Service Medal (Ray Hooley)

We had a bit of a skirmish, that was unsuccessful and it was decided that there would be another battle, this was about October 1918. We were ready just behind the line where I was checking the water and so on when I discovered that my Tank had a broken fan belt. I thought we'd get left behind. Somehow one of the Officers came along with a spare and I just managed to get it fitted in time. We were parked behind a battery of 18 pounders who had been firing intermittently all night. Suddenly the tempo started to increase, so we knew it couldn't be long before the battle started. Soon we moved off and as we drove passed the battery, one engine stopped. Luckily by coupling one engine to the other I managed to get it started again. I crept around the front of the battery as they fired over our heads and went out into no man's land. I felt rather nervous as I had to pick my way between both British and German wounded. We negotiated them and soon got past the heavy Tanks and started off towards our objective, a village on top of a hill called Premont, I think, I'm not too sure. We could see it and there was a valley just before it. We dropped down into the valley; I could see my right hand Tank as we were in a diamond formation. The left hand Tank was a bit higher up. Suddenly the left hand

This Whippet received a direct hit from German artillery whilst supporting Canadian infantry at Le Fresnoy in 1918. Both crew members were killed instantly and the wreckage is now a photo opportunity for an American 'Doughboy'

one stopped as he got a track blown off. I shot around him and turned the Tank sideways on so that the left hand gunner could pick off the German battery, who were in an orchard. Suddenly there was a bang and I knew nothing else until I woke up, I must have been knocked out, I suppose. I was still sitting in the driving seat with the wheel in my hand. The Tank door was open and the officer had vanished, the other gunner was dead at the side of the gun. I could only see out of one eye, it was nothing much, just a scratch from a ricochet I think. To be perfectly truthful I was scared stiff as a sitting Tank is a sitting target and I shot straight out of my seat and made myself as small as possible in a nearby shell hole. There were none of our troops around and I didn't know where the Germans were. I lay low and dabbed my eye with some iodine. Eventually I summoned up enough courage and crawled along a sunken road and found some our infantry and my officer Captain May managed to find me. I went to the first aid tent where I found my pal from one of the other Tanks had been wounded in the arm. I was taken in an ambulance to a railhead where I was given the job of looking after a man who'd been shot through the head. He was completely unconscious, but had the strength of ten men. I almost had to sit on him to keep him still. We got to where there was a railway which Jerry was bombing, but we got through. Eventually I got to the 5th General Hospital and I was there for about 6 weeks, it wasn't really very serious, but I suppose it could have been. I often laugh about my time there. Being an outpatient there we used to go to a hut in the grounds to get food. Well, food was a bit scarce so a couple of us used to go around twice. Somehow they tumbled to this, so they started issuing tickets which you had to hand in when you went in. I managed to pinch a few tickets, which kept us going for a few days.

Harry Emans, seated without his hat at the front of the rowing boat. This photograph was taken in 1919 on the moat of the Schloss at Kendenich, south west of Cologne (Ray Hooley)

Male Mk V L 9 on peace keeping duties in Cologne in 1919. Harry Emans was the driver of tank L 7

31

At the end of the war I stayed on and went to Germany, Cologne, with a different lot, a different Tank battalion. All my pals were demobbed and I was on my own. I still remember my first crew; we were only together for Arras and Passchendaele and not after that. We soon got split, you don't stay long as a crew, it's the way it is in the army, you have to do as you're told. I never kept in touch with them as I should have done. You say 'Where do you come from?' and they say Glasgow, Leeds or Bradford, but you don't think at the time to get their addresses.

Sergeant Harry Emans waits at Cologne Railway Station for a train to take him back to be demobbed in England. When interviewed in 1987 he still had his ash plant stick and his chainmail mask (Ray Hooley)

78907 Pte. Valentine 'Val' Field

Aged 86 when interviewed

Motor Transport Service 1916
Tank Corps 'E' Battalion 1916-18

I joined the Motor Transport Service because I was told that they were very short of drivers and I'd held a licence for about three years. I was 18 years of age and so I joined up and went to Grove Park, this would have been in 1916. We did the standard Army Service Corps squad drill to turn us into soldiers before we had anything to do with the motors, but before long I was transferred into the Tank Corps. At this time it was known as the Heavy Battalion Motor Machine Gun Corps and I went

A typical scene showing drivers from the Motor Transport Section of the Army Service Corps with their lorry

straight off to Bovington. There was 250 of us, because they were making up five battalions at Bovington. We were struck off, about two days after we'd arrived, into a group of about 60 and we marched off 'A' lines in the camp. This consisted of three rows of huts which were empty at the time. We arrived at the old Guard Room where there was a Colonel, several Majors, other officers, Sergeant Majors and Sergeants. We were handed over to them and stuck off into three groups of 20, 'A', 'B' and 'C' companies to be trained as Tank drivers. We each went off to our respective lines and the next afternoon a party arrived from the Motor Machine Gun Corps which had been all but disbanded as they was trained for motorbikes and sidecars with Vickers Guns and, of course, they couldn't jump the trenches. For days afterwards there were groups arriving from practically every regiment of the British army. In the mean time the old soldiers that had been there to greet us, mainly Drill Sergeants from infantry regiments, were there for just one reason, to knock it into us on the square, and they did just that! For two months, while the regiment was being built up, we did nothing but square bashing. If we had any spare time, instead of a game of football, we'd have a route-march. Physical training, square bashing and route-marching were our rations! Eventually the day came when they said that they were going to form the crews and they lined us up into two ranks. The Divisional Commander came and there was the Sergeant Major with his stick. He said 'From here to the right, eight men struck off for a crew, quick march'. The Officer standing by then took charge of them and they were his Tank crew. Of the men, like myself, who had been sent down with the purpose of being trained as drivers, we were anywhere. Fortunately, I was the only one in our eight, but some eights consisted of two or three drivers from the Motor Transport Service and others had none! The officers took their crews off to the parade ground where they took their particulars and designated their duties in the crew. To the first man in our front rank, they said to him 'You'll be a driver' He was a driver, he drove a horse and cart, he was a butchers roundsman. The man behind him was a ginger pop merchant and he was to be second driver and gearsman. The other gearsman was a jeweller's apprentice engraver. The remainder were split up into two machine gunners or six pound gunners for either side leaving myself as odd man out. I was informed that I would do the duties of runner, combined with Batman, I refused the Batmans post. Anyway, the next week we were detailed for courses. Everyone had to go and look at the notice boards to see what courses they would be on. I ran my eyes down it expecting to see myself on the driver's course, but I wasn't there. I went through everything until saw a small course at the end which was 'pigeons'. These were our wireless at the time, our means of communication and each Tank carried three pigeons. Later, on one occasion, we did release one when we had a temporary break down. If the record runs true, he did well, as he was booked in six minutes after leaving the Tank, not bad considering.

Pigeon post worked well enough in theory, but in practice these animals were not suited to life in a tank (The Tank Museum, Bovington)

Anyway, I was on this course for pigeons, but all I knew about pigeons was that they made jolly good pies and puddings, I should know as I had carried a catapult from the age of eight, right up until I joined the army. We were taught how and when to feed the birds, how to write the messages and how to fasten them to their legs. We had to make sure that they were hungry before we released them and then they would fly home for their grub. That lasted about five days and that was the end of that.

Next, after the pigeons, I was sent on a cross country map reading course followed by a revolver course, a gas course, a grenade course, everything in fact except Tanks. When there was nothing else left to be sent on I eventually made it onto the Tank course and I was very lucky as I came out with one of the very few first class tickets that they'd dished out. I finished up getting the drivers job after all. It was a wonderful experience to finally get into a Tank. I looked around and there I was sitting at the front with the officer beside me. There were the two Gunners on either side and the two gearsmen were on a seat over the top of the gearbox where they could get at the gear levers on either side, this was necessary for sharp turning. You could do a little variation with the levers in the front, but you couldn't turn. When you wanted to do a turn, you banged your fist on the engine cover and held up your fist to indicate neutral. If you banged and held up one finger, that was first gear, two fingers was for second. Whilst we were practicing our driving, the gunners were more or less spectators, but they were where they'd have to be in action. When their turn came and we had to do the live firing, we had to drive as we would if it were battle conditions, everything all closed down. After about an hour's run you didn't need an overcoat, it was so hot inside. There was no ventilation and no extractor fans in the old originals, you had to be tough. We did this training where we had to deliberately ditch the car and then we got the order to attach the old unditching beam. Sometimes we ditched it rather too well for practice, but we always got through, you couldn't always choose you spot. It was a thing that had to be done and had to be

This female Mk IV has done its best to escape, but it looks as though the unditching beam was unsuccessful in this instance

done in a hurry. If you were in action there would be other people on the other side, the enemy, who would also be interested in your welfare at the time, so you had to be right on the job. We had overalls to wear in the Tanks, but depending on the weather, if it was hot, we just wore trousers and a shirt; you were just one mass of sweat. Later on, I had an old beret that I used to wear. It had come from one of the French Alpine Chasseurs, who became Tanks. I scrounged it off them as it was very awkward for a driver to use a steel helmet, you had to get your head close to the flaps, the beret was unofficial of course. In the lockers at the sides of the Tank were quite a number of things including iron rations, which consisted of biscuits, Bully Beef and Maconochies. There were also bags of raisins, which were in great demand. You'd soak the biscuits into a pulp, put a dollop of raisins in the middle, put the lot into the tail of your shirt, boil it up and you'd have bread pudding, this meant you always had a washed shirt too! There was always a big torch and a few other bits in these lockers, but apart from that there wasn't room for much. The cover over the gearbox consisted of a flat top, which you could open. Inside was a complete toolbox, everything was inlaid, everything in its place, the 3/8th spanner went in the 3/8th space, they were all different sizes and different lengths. There were screwdrivers, adjustable spanners, everything you needed, it was a lovely kit. The top shut down and in the Mk IVs that was used as a seat for the two gearsmen. The Mk V was similar in that the gunners would rest on it when we were travelling. I take my hat off to the old Daimler engine, it was very good and we had only two breakdowns. I remember getting tied in a knot putting a new belt on, they were the old leather belts and you put them on with a screwdriver and a screw, not nice rubber ones like today. It gave me a dead leg, it was a devil of a job, standing on your head in cramped quarters, you had to be a conjurer to do some of those jobs. I had an advantage over a lot of the people because long before I'd left school I would haunt my fathers workshop, especially in the winter. He was in charge of all the mechanical stuff on this estate and he had a big workshop. On a Saturday, if it was wet and cold, I'd go up there and he'd teach me all sorts, a bit of Blacksmithing, that sort of thing. I had this advantage that meant that I could turn my hand to most things when I went into the Army. Most of the men that came in from the Motor Transport Corps could drive, but believe me, half of them hardly knew why you changed a sparking plug, they could drive, but had no idea about taking things to pieces. Later on, if someone wasn't pulling their weight, we had a remedy for that. We handed him a grease-gun, there were 72 points around the outside of a Tank that needed greasing. It wasn't like a modern grease-gun where you push and its spring loaded, a tube came out of the end which was threaded, you undid a quarter gas thread plug and took it out of the end of the roller. You then screwed the gun in until you couldn't screw any more, it was the most unpleasant job that there was in the Tank Corps. I guarantee that if you did them all and did them properly, that was a real punishment. Inside there were 21 grease-cups which you had to screw down. The Workshop Officer would come and look around and if he saw a grease-cup only half way down and loose, he'd tell you off. You had to know when he was coming and be ready for him, unless you had a good excuse you'd be in his black books. The driver was responsible for keeping the dirt out of the carburettor and so on, but otherwise there wasn't a great deal of maintenance. I take my hat off to the old Daimler engines.

After the square bashing had been done, we were regarded as soldiers; the courses had been to make us mechanical soldiers. Now we'd got through all of that we were ready and we were sent off in early June to Wool Camp. I distinctly remember that the Middlesex Boys band played us down to the station to the tune of 'When we've wound up the watch on the Rhine'. I'll always remember that, because after Cambrai, when we'd lost so much we began to wonder just who was winding up who's watch! When we first arrived in France we spent three or four days in a camp at Le Harve waiting for the Tanks to arrive so that we could get stocked up and ready. We went off to a place up in Belgium between Poperinge and the front line, it was a place called Oosthoek Wood. Once there we hid under the trees, we were about three or four Kilometres behind the lines. Fortunately the part that we used was a plantation where the trees had been planted in rows and we were able to get in between them, making it quite easy to camouflage the Tanks. We did get the occasional shell, but nobody was ever killed there. When we met the Infantry, we got mixed reactions. Some were delighted to see us, but the Australians hated our guts, because they said that the Tanks drew shell fire and that meant they got it too. They said that they would rather do without us, but they altered their tune before the end of the war. While we were in the woods, we couldn't do any training as there was no room. We could only do stuff that we could manage under cover. It was chiefly familiarizing ourselves with the use of the guns, stripping down and that sort of thing. If there was a jam under fire, you needed to be able to rectify it quickly. We did a lot of observations on German balloons. They were like our barrage balloons that we used in the second war, except they had a basket on them with an observer in and they could see for miles, we had the same thing. The time finally came that we moved up, I think it was the 31st July. The night previous, we moved forward to a position somewhere near to the 18pdr gun sites. We were then in easier distance to the front line for the jump off point. We were so slow when in motion that we had to be very close when things started. When we started up the barrage also began and that deadened the noise from our engines so that the Germans couldn't hear us, but they had no need to be afraid as we were in the wrong place and we sank in. My own particular Tank *(E43 Eldorado commanded by Lt. Bayliss)* didn't make it and several others didn't either, they just sank into the mud and had to be recovered later *(Due to German artillery fire, recovery proved impossible. Eldorado actually stayed in-situ until being recovered and scrapped soon after the war)*. The whole of the thing, considering the Tanks, was just a washout. If you've ever played cricket you'll know that as you walk out, you get a little tingle down your spine, well, that's what I got when we went off into action, everyone else in the crew felt more or less the same. The officers were briefed before the battle; they had the maps and so on. Perhaps if there was an NCO in the crew they would discuss the plan with them, but otherwise we just went off and did what the officer told us.

Val Fields Female Mk IV tank, the original E43 Eldorado. Seen here after the battle, ditched in a shell hole in the middle of the village of Langemark and left in-situ until after the war

This picture demonstrates the entire problem with the Third Battle of Ypres. Huge armoured 28ton tanks sent onto ground that wouldn't support the weight of a man

After we got another Tank, we gave it a clean up and a while later we went back in again another ten kilometres further south. The ground was very much the same again and very few of our Tanks actually got into action. After this, they all thought we were no good in the mud, so we went off further south onto the Somme. We did small jobs here and there and we did one or two larger jobs, sometimes only a company's strength. We worked our way down for the next few months until early in November we found ourselves in front of Cambrai. By November, we'd all developed into our jobs and we had a very affective crew. When we needed to start, the officer or me yelled for the starting handle and there were four willing chaps got hold of it and they knew how to spin it around. It took a bit of doing in the cold weather; a 105hp was a bit different from starting an Austin Seven! We were a pretty efficient crew. We got down to Havrincourt Wood and we were two or three days there getting ready for Cambrai. It was a terrific wood where we all congregated; one battalion went into a nearby village and drove their Tanks into some of the empty houses, allowing the roofs to collapse onto them as camouflage and they were ready for the big day.

Our officer *(2nd Lt. C.E. Windle)* had all the dope on what was ahead for us and our battalion had a couple of spares Tanks. The seventh, 'G' battalion were laying close by us and they required some help, so our battalion loaned them some Tanks, one of which I drove. The other Tank was driven by a friend of mine who was a gunner *(Gnr. W.L.M. Francis)*. His Tank got knocked out early, they took out the guns with them when they had to get out. There was a plane come over and in those days, they used to fly very low, so he was going to have a go at it. The officer told him not to be such a so-and-so fool, he'd get his head blown off and that he should get down. When this plane came over again Francis poked the gun up and let fly and forced the plane down, he got an M.M. and a months leave for that! I was lucky with my own Tank, the only problem being that the Germans took the exhaust pipe off it which meant it made a devil of a row, I can tell you. Anyhow, we all got home safe and sound for the evening and then got ready for the next day. It was a difficult job fighting in a Tank, you got thrown about a bit, but each of you had something to grab hold of. The Gunners had got their guns and they just braced themselves in various positions after they'd found out which was the best. It was very uncomfortable, but the worst thing was the heat. After you'd been running for an hour, what with the smell of the cordite and the engine fumes, there were no extractor fans the only outlet was the opening for the gun. The conditions were far from being ideal; when I looked at the name on the outside of the Tank I wondered where we'd got it from. We were E battalion and so our name had to start with 'E', so it was called Eldorado, it was far from it! Anyway, we achieved several of the objectives that were detailed to us. The problem was communications with the other Tanks. It was done by runner; there was no wireless or anything, no signals at all. Later on they did put a semaphore arm on top of the Tanks so that you could signal to one another, but the first time you used your unditching beam, it just swept it away, so that wasn't much of a success. These semaphore arms were OK, but they would get broken off. The ground at Cambrai was perfect, The Hindenburg Line was more of less a rest camp for any German regiments, because they knew jolly well that no infantry on earth could penetrate anything like 50 to 100 yards of barbed wire, even the Butterflies had to fly sideways through it! The ground there was dry and it was good travelling. The Germans were very scared, most of the Regiments hadn't seen Tanks before and it came as a real surprise to them in that particular sector. They never thought anything would ever come to them there; most of the trenches were empty. There wasn't a great deal of opposition for the first two or three days. There was one place in front of my old battalion where the Germans stayed put and they nearly annihilated the entire battalion, but otherwise the Germans were very scared of us and retreated. We didn't see much of the Cavalry for the first couple of

German Anti-Tank cables and concrete tank traps

days, the infantry were making such good progress that we thought they were just letting them carry on. They hadn't had the opposition they'd expected. On the third or fourth day, the cavalry arrived, but barbed wire and horses don't mix up very well. They just trotted about in people's way and they were more of a hindrance than a help. Aircraft were very scarce on both sides, one or two Germans came over and one or two of ours did, but there was nothing much. We didn't see any aerial combat, like we had in other places. The German air force seemed to be no help to their army at all. Anyway, on the first day of Cambrai the General chose H battalion and rode into battle in a Tank called Hilda, which was one of the very first Tanks to get ditched, so the poor fellow had to get out and walk. When he got out of the Tank they were ditched and not in a very advanced position, things had all gone past them and I don't quite know what happened to him after that. In years to come, whenever we met any H battalion men at the driving school or whatever, we'd kid them a bit and always say 'Give them a bit extra, they come from H battalion, they even ditched the General'. Our Tank was the old Eldorado II and it was out of commission after the first day, but there were one or two Tanks that had to go in again on the fourth day. There were these three officers talking, our Officer, Windle, and two of the other Battalion Officers. Anyway, the other two of them had got the Military Cross and our fellow hadn't got

Female Mk IV C47 Conqueror on the battlefield at the end of Cambrai

anything. They said to him 'Now's your chance' and we took one of these other officers Tanks over, our own crew, but his Tank. We went in on the fourth day and he got his M.C. This fellows Tank we'd borrowed broke down at one point and we had to work on it. There was an abandoned German battery placed close by, so the Officer left the second driver and me in the Tank to fix it and went with the rest of the crew into the shelter of this German battery. We'd been working for ten minutes and the officer sent one of the men across to see if we'd finished, we said 'No, of course not, we shall be some time yet', he kept on sending this fellow back and forth. Anyway my mate said to me 'Do you want a drink of tea Field?' and I said yes. I had just finished bolting up this bit that I was doing and my mate had just two or three nuts to put on when this officer raised hell at me because I went across to the shelter to get a cup of tea. He chased me back to the Tank and five minutes later I went back over and the officer shouted 'Are you back here again?' and I said 'Yes, I need some help to swing it over, we're ready to start up'. This other feller gave me a cup of tea quick and do you know, when we came out of the dugout the Officer deliberately knocked it with his elbow and knocked it over. The officers weren't all bad, I remember our section Captain, Captain Griffiths; I'd loved to have met him after the war or indeed at any time. There was also our old Company Sergeant Major, he couldn't march very well because he'd been wounded in the leg whilst serving with the Buffs, but he was a gentleman, he was Sergeant Major Carpenter, later on he was our Regimental Sergeant Major. As regards our Company Commander, A.H. Gatehouse, later on he was a Major General in the last war. Anyway, as I was saying, we got the Tank going again and we didn't really do anything outstanding that day; we just did what we were supposed to do. At the end of the day, we were just ready to pull back when we saw an officer in a trench. He was signalling to us and shouting 'Over there, over there!' I got out and went over to see this bloke and he pointed out a German strongpoint that must have been built six months before. It was one of these sandbagged efforts, machine gun fire against it was useless and we'd got a female Tank. The only thing I could do was drive straight up to it and put one track over, put it into neutral and did a curve over it and back into gear and pulled out again. As we pulled out I saw a bit of clothing coming around, hanging off the tracks and then a mans forearm and hand came around in the track, that had finished them off.

The last I saw of the old Eldorado II was when the Royal Engineers had made some excavations on a ridge and I had to drive this Tank along, with others, into these holes along the ridge. They sandbagged them all round to make strong-points along the ridge, so that if the Germans did counter attack, that would be as far as they got. After Cambrai we held about a third of the ground we'd taken, that's all we had afterwards. After Cambrai we went to our winter quarters to a place close to Albert. From there we went down to a place called Tincourt close to Peronne and we were there on the 21st March 1918 when the big German counter-offensive started and we went forwards to meet them in a new Tank. There was such a dense fog that we just couldn't see anything. You could see a man, just a shape moving in the fog at a dozen or about 20 yards away, but you daren't fire because it may have been one of our own. We withdrew a bit, because they were pushing and then we withdrew a bit more and at the finish we came to a river which we couldn't get across. The bridge was too narrow and it was mined, there was this Royal Engineers officer with a man standing back at about 200 yards on guard ready to blow the bridge up. He said he would give us a quarter of an hour. All I wanted to do was to push in one sponson, which meant taking out a series of bolts so that you could slide the sponson in and get over the bridge. This RE officer said 'No, I'll give you just a quarter of an hour'. We thought, what are we going to do; we couldn't leave the Tank for the Germans. The officer said that he would take the rest of the crew over the bridge and he left me to dispose of the Tank. I got a spanner out, I had the engine running, and with this spanner I undid the pipe from the carburettor which spilt out plenty of petrol and petrol vapour. I didn't smoke so I hadn't got a match or a light, so I stood off to one side with my arm around the door and I fired my revolver in. There was such a whoosh, if I'd been stood in the doorway it would have blown me over. The Tank went up in flames and I jumped out and ran across the bridge and the RE officer never blew the bridge, not for another two hours! Not until this fellow came running along shouting 'They're just behind me, they're just behind me!' We could see this group back behind him some distance, they were Jerry's. The officer blew the bridge and when this group got to it, they were our own fellows! This place was called Brie where we blew the Tank up. The armour plate of the Tanks was all right against bullets, but not against a shell. The armour was non-existent, it would break like ice. A field gun today would need to be a direct hit with armour-piercing to do anything to a Tank nowadays, but back then an 18pdr shell would just go through, burst inside and do a hell of a lot of damage. That's how a lot of them were wiped out, a shell bursting inside, almost anything would break through. It was nice to hear bullets rattling like a hailstorm on the outside

They seemed indestructible, but artillery fire could turn a tank to scrap with a single shot

when they really got annoyed with you. The Germans had an armour piercing rifle. It was a single shot, but otherwise it was almost identical to the Anti-Tank rifle issued to the British army in the last war *(The 1937 .55 calibre or 13.9mm Boyes Anti-Tank Rifle)* I only know of one case when one of these German anti-Tank rifle bullets came through the side and I'll tell you, the Devil himself must have fired it. The Daimler engine was a dry sump; it would pump the oil back into an oblong oil tank at the end of the engine. A pipe came down underneath that with an 'S' bend on it. This incorporated the dynamo switch, so that you couldn't start your engine without turning your oil on, when you switched the ignition on it turned the oil over, automatically. This German anti-Tank bullet came through the side of the Tank and cut this pipe in two. The first thing we knew about it was bang, bang, bang and one of the big ends came through the side of the engine!

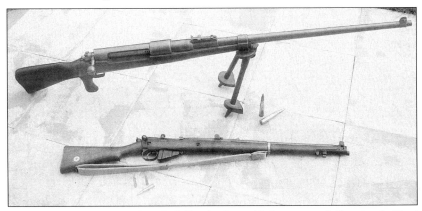

The huge German Mauser 13.2mm Tank-Gewehr, the worlds first purpose built anti-tank rifle. A standard British .303 Lee Enfield rifle has been placed alongside for scale

The next thing, we were scattered around with the infantry, paired off and used as machine gunners, we had no Tanks at all. When we got back together, we got a different crew, I knew what happened to a couple of my old crew, but whatever happened to the others, I just don't know. We eventually got Mk V Tanks in place of the Mk IVs. With the new Mk V there was none of that banging on the engine covers and holding fingers up, it was all one man control. It was heaven compared to the Mk IV. Apart from manoeuvrability the old Mk IV was just as good; they would climb anything that a Mk V would. It was in a Mk V that I got blown up. I was going away on leave two days later and so at the time I wasn't actually in a Tank crew at all. The Oxfordshire Regiment came along and they were going to attack this lovely valley about a Kilometre across, in the middle of it was this Château. Everything looked lovely, the artillery were just behind the ridge and they had shelled the old Château. It was just a pile of brick dust, but what they didn't know was that underneath the Château was a cellar just as high as the building and it was packed with machine guns. The machine guns had a good field of fire, about four or five-hundred yards either way. The poor old Ox and Bucks came along and the officer realised that it was going to be suicide; he left and joined our regiment. So, they had a new officer and no Tank, we had a Tank and no officer. I met an officer at the artillery battery; I had two gunners with me. This officer came to us and took the particulars of the gunners. He said to the first one, 'What's your name' and he said 'Parker', the officer said 'Right, you'll be my Number 1'. The other gunner said that he knew nothing about guns. I said to him, 'You've got a first class ticket!' and I grabbed at his inside pocket and yanked his paybook out. Well, the back page was gone, torn out. I said to the officer 'I'll do it, can't I go?' That's how I got mixed up in it all. Anyway, we went off to this Château and the other Tank came in from the other side and we soon could see where the German fire was coming from. We didn't fire until we got within a couple of hundred yards, and we could see it was coming from ground level. We gave them some crossfire with the six pounders and at 200yrds you could put one down the barrel of the German machine gun. We carried on and in a short while there was shirt came out on the end of a rifle, they'd packed it in. The infantry had advanced when we opened up and so they were soon there and this sergeant and half of his platoon went into the cellar. Presently the came back out with bottles of wine and all sorts of other stuff. The officer said to him 'Did you find any Germans in there' and he nodded and said 'Yes Sir, there were about a dozen of them skulking in there'. The officer says 'Well, where are they then?' the sergeant replies 'They're still in there Sir'. The officer understood what had happened. We had a drink of this wine and soon this runner came up to tell us that there was some strong opposition at the tip of a wood nearby, so we set off for it. The Germans were getting near the end at this point and they knew it. What they used to do if they had a strong point was drop back overnight and as they went they would dig holes in the ground and drop a 5.9 shell in with a special cap on it. Men could walk over it and be all right, but if a limber or a Tank ran over it the 5.9 would go up and you'd had it. We were there firing away and we hit one of these 5.9s. Everything was a bit unclear for a couple of hours afterwards, as I'd passed out. I came round and it was getting near dusk, I was lying on the floor of the Tank and then I passed out again. I woke up for a second time and it was dark, there were no lights on in the Tank and there was no firing going on from either side. I tried to get up and I found that I couldn't, my leg was somehow tangled around the mounting of the gun. I called out to see if there was anyone else in there, but there was no answer. I could see a dim shape lying over the gearbox, it turned out later that it was one of the gunners, he was dead. I laid there for some time and struggled, but couldn't get out. Out of the corner of my eye I saw a flicker, there was something under the driver's seat, it was a tiny flame. I thought to myself, it's going to catch fire and I struggled, I was getting desperate. Then I felt something move on my foot and then there was a grunt. I yelled out to Parker, the other gunner, and he moved again and I was able to move my legs, he'd been lying unconscious across my legs. He then got up, so I jumped up and I grabbed one of the eight fire extinguishers, the old brass Pyrenes. I put the fire out and had a look around, the driver was dead and the other gunner was also dead. The door on the other side was open, the officer must have thought we were all dead and gone and left us. Rather than disturb the chap who was lying there dead, I went across and opened the door on our side. The Germans had been waiting and made a mistake by opening fire on the open door, so I was able to hook it back and fasten it up. We said 'We'll give them something to remember us by' and we put about a dozen rounds into this building they were in and I don't think there were any left alive, we could see two or three of them at ground level. We were only about 50 yards away, that was deadly with a six pounder and he was a good gunner too. There was no reply, so we waited a bit and said we best get out of the other side. I decided I'd belt off about 100 yards and see if there was anywhere that we could get into and then I'll stop and wait. I said to him 'If you don't make it, I'll come back for you'. We shook hands; we didn't know what was going to happen. I shot off out and about 80 yards down I found a natural hole in the ground and I flopped into it. I looked around and I could hear old Parker running down towards me. We both got in the hole just as some firing began. I decided that there was only one thing for it; we'd just have to wait until it got dark. When it got dark I stuck Parkers tin hat up in one place, nothing happened, so I went along and put it up in another place, nothing happened, so we got up and started to wander back. We must have been right at the junction with the French line because we could see this French sentry moving. He walked up between two clumps of bushes and then went back again, so I got behind one of the bushes. When he came back, he had his rifle down, so I grabbed his rifle and pushed my revolver into his ribs and told him in my best French that we were British Tank Corps. He was all right and he shouted out in a string of French I didn't understand and we went in. The French gave us some wine and the officer said that a British Tank officer and one other man, both wounded had passed by them several hours before. We finished our wine and went back along the line to our own quarters. On the way we saw a Tank and I knocked on the outside and shouted to tell them who we were. They were pleased to see us as they thought we'd been done in. From the ridge further back, they'd seen our Tank go up in flames and they were pleased to see that two of us had made it back. I told them what the French had said about the officer and other man, that made four survivors and then the two dead, was the whole crew of six. After this I came home and joined the 21st Battalion and got a fortnights leave.

I take my hat off to the old Daimler engines; I would have been quite satisfied with a Mk IV with the Daimler engine and epicyclic one man control gearing. The Mk V had the 150hp Ricardo engine, but it no more ability, just a little extra speed. If it was tuned up properly, you'd maybe get 6 MPH out of it, whereas we'd be lucky to get 4 MPH out of the Mk IV. Near the end of the war, they'd got these Tanks ready for 1918-19, Mediums they called them. The Medium A Whippet was the first Medium Tank. Next was the Medium B, a lovely looking thing, they knocked the horsepower down and put the engine in the back. It was almost impossible to do anything to the engine as it was in a little partition in the back.

The Medium B, a disappointing tank created by the otherwise excellent designer and engineer Major Walter Gordon Wilson (The Tank Museum, Bovington)

They were no good at all, you had a hell of a job to start it and when it did start it was just as likely to pack up on you. They were never issued. Next they made the Medium C with a 150hp Ricardo engine. After the war I had been using a Mk V over in Dublin and we came back for some sports at Bovington, the Southern Command Sports, as I used to be a runner. I brought this team over and they said to me there is a driving competition. I thought to myself I can win this, I didn't think I was second to anybody, I was confident that I was as good as the next one. We got up there and there were these Medium Cs, we'd never seen the damn things before,

Described as the best tank of its era, the Medium C. Created in Lincoln by the staff of William Foster and Co Ltd

so me and my mate had a look around them and we came away with the silver cup. Afterwards, instead of sending us back to Dublin, they said to themselves, we've got the chaps we want here and they put us into the Naval and Military tournament, driving a Medium C for an exhibition of Tank driving, it was a lovely little Tank. I don't think they got as much speed out of a Medium C as they should have done. It was a lighter Tank, 150hp, and they should have had at least 12-15 MPH out of it, but it didn't. You were lucky if you'd get 10MPH, they were only designed for 8 MPH, but you could get 10MPH if you tickled about with them.

The Victory March through London on the 19th July 1919. Men of the Tank Corps march proudly along followed by their new tank, the Medium C, one of which is being driven by Val Field

They were in use with the Tank Corps for a number of years until the Vickers came along and pushed them out. To finish up with I did the City of London Victory March on the 19th July 1919, I'll always remember that as it was my Mothers birthday. I wouldn't have missed joining up it for a thousand pounds, my only regret was that I was one of the first bunch that helped form the 5th Battalion and I left them exactly a month before the armistice and I never went on the Rhine with them.

Val Field aged 86 and still proud to wear the Tank Corps blazer and regimental tie

91686 Pte. William 'Mac' Francis M.M.

Aged 89 when interviewed

Tank Corps 'E' Battalion 1916-18

I was the lowest rank in the British army when I joined, a private or a gunner. My army number was 91686, I was C Company of the 5th Battalion of the Tank Corps. When I first joined up I was in Kitcheners Army, I went to Shrewsbury and saw the Colonel there, the recruiting colonel I suppose he would be, he was a very nice chap. 'Take a seat' he said 'Sit down and make yourself comfortable' this was unusual for the army. He asked me what I wanted to join and I told him that I fancied the Mechanical Transport Section of the Army Service Corps. 'Do you really, what makes you fancy that' he said. I told him that I was used to driving cars in the grocery trade. We were tea specialists, I could buy tea just by looking at it, I didn't have to taste it to tell if it would make a good cup of tea. Anyway, the officer asked me what car I'd driven and I told him it was a Model T Ford. 'Good God, that's not a car, it's an orange box!' he said. So I told him that I'd also driven a lorry and he asked what kind, I said that it was a Straker Squire. He asked me how long I'd been driving and if I could do running repairs. I told him that I'd been driving for about six months and that I'd

A 1912 Straker Squire lorry as driven by William Francis before the war

done a course on repairs before I'd started. He looked at me for a while and sighed and then said 'Hmm, no, you're a bit too tall for what I want'. Anyway, he carried on and said to me 'What would you do if you were driving a lorry and you come to a steep hill. You've tried it in first and second and you've tried it in the bottom gear and it still won't go up, what would you do?' I told him that I'd look for another route if it was so steep, but that wasn't the answer he wanted. I knew what answer he was after, I'd been told about this other chap the day before. I said 'Well let me see. I could put it into reverse and go up that way. It's a much lower gear' He looked at me and said 'That's a good answer, but I don't know, you're still too tall for what I want'. I was about 5'11". Finally he said 'All right, I will take a chance with you, dismissed'. The next thing I got a rail warrant to go to Bovington Camp. It was midnight and I arrived at this little Railway Station at Wool, it was pitch-dark. I found somebody and said to them, 'What sort of place is this?' I still thought I'd be driving army lorries, I had no idea. I suppose the Recruiting Colonel at Shrewsbury knew, but he didn't tell me. I got a good night's sleep and the next morning I got up and went out and saw these iron clad monsters going up and down over sand dunes, tree stumps and barbed wire. I said to myself 'What the hell have I let myself in for, this is not going to be a cushy job driving lorries'. Of course these things were some of the original Tanks. I'd never heard of them at all, very few would have done, only those on the camp I expect. I couldn't work it out, they looked like battleships on the land! I got back in for breakfast after PT and then I found out what it was, it was the Tanks and I suddenly realised why the Colonel had thought I was too tall for what he wanted, you had to bend down very low to get into a Tank. Anyway, I managed to fit in all right. We started doing courses and I did a gas course first. I was in there with an old fashioned gas mask on when I saw the brass buttons on my tunic suddenly went black, just like that, good Lord I thought, I'd never even heard of gas, you see. I was just a country lad from Oswestry and I'd never been out, I was a bit on the shy side. I was only 16 or 17 years old, I could never speak to girls, I never smoked or drank and I'd never even been to a theatre. We weren't very well organised, there must have been 500 other chaps arrive, perhaps more, I'm not sure. Anyway, they weren't very organised because I dodged the PT parades, other parades and the route marches with full pack. I must have dodged them all for about two months, but I always used to go to battalion headquarters to see if my name was down for any courses, because you'd get booked if you missed them. For about two months, me and my pal Jim

Kay from Lancashire used to go around. I'd have a broom and he'd have a bucket. We would go into the YMCA hut or the Wesleyan Soldiers hut and pretend we were on fatigue duty. If the Military Police came in we'd be brushing the floor or picking up the cigarette ends and they never questioned us, it was unbelievable! You'd never go on a PT first parade at 8 o'clock in the morning because they counted them and always then expected the same number. When I first saw my name down for a course, it was for the pigeon course. I remember the first line of the instruction from the sergeant was 'Never handle the pigeons with greasy hands' and I suppose the course lasted for only about a week. We learnt how to write a message and pin it to the pigeons leg and you could send a message back to headquarters in case the Tank got knocked out or stuck, I forget if I passed or not, I can just remember that first instruction. The next course was Morse Code and I was a washout at it, I think I got just 5 marks out of 100 for it. I couldn't get to grips with Morse Code. Next, I went for a re-

Early 1918, Gunner Francis on the right poses for a photograph with one of his brothers. Note the ribbon for his Military Medal and cloth 'E' Battalion shoulder flashes (Philippe Gorczynski)

volver course and my word, I was pretty good at that, I'd never fired a gun before and I got two bull's-eyes out of five. I was 'T-Total', so I'd got a very steady hand and I think I was the best of the lot that week. I got better and better and I thought by Jove, I'd better watch out, the Tanks are pretty bad, but I don't want to end up being a sniper at any cost. After I'd got several more bulls and was doing very well, I deliberately deteriorated my firing, so I wasn't picked out to be a sniper. I then did a Lewis Gun course, I remember that after about a weeks training we had to run with a Lewis Gun about 50 yards, then drop down quickly and fire about 50 rounds. I was a bit of a Devil really and I wasn't getting the gun down on the ground quick enough, it was always, 'Francis, Francis, drop that gun down quicker, your too slow and you'll get shot before you've turned around!'. He made me go back round and do it again, so I did and I banged the gun down so hard on some hard ground that it broke the front part of the Lewis Gun off. I thought 'Oh, no, I'm in for a Court Marshall now', but I wasn't. Anyway, I went through the Lewis Gun and I was pretty good at that, just like I was with the revolver. As I told you I had dodged things a bit for a couple of months and then I got put onto the Tank Course. I was going over Bovington Camp, up and down for the first week, I wasn't the driver, I was Lewis Gunner. You had evacuate the Tank, learn to dodge the bumps with your head and get in and out quickly in so many seconds, we must have been doing this for about a month I would think. There were about 20 of us in the same hut, but at this time we weren't in Tank crews, that happened much later. I remember the Welshman in charge of our hut Sergeant Evans, quite a good chap he was too. I can member Sergeant Major Car-

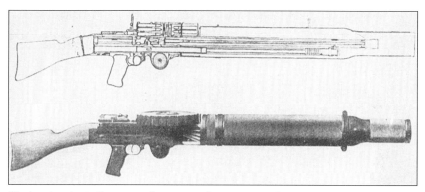

The American Lewis Gun, an excellent weapon, but not universally appreciated amongst the men of the Tank Corps

penter, unusually for a Sergeant Major he was a bit bandy, he must have been in the Horse Guards or something. He was very aged, he must have been 50 or 60 years old I suppose, very old for a Sergeant Major. He still came out to France with us though, the Sergeant Major usually had a cushy time and wouldn't come out for the fighting. When we did finally get crewed up I was with Jim Kay, Bernard Gallaher from Ayr in Scotland, he was an ex-chauffeur, he's passed on now. There was Taffy Jones, he used to sing, he was in the church choir at home, he was from Abersoch. There was Tuck, he was a Cockney, I could tell you a funny story about Tuck and his boiled eggs for breakfast *(304482 Pte. A.J. Tuck 15th Battn. Tank Corps. Killed in action 9th August 1918)*. Then there was my pal Jim Kay, he never came through it *(91520 Pte. James Lord Kay 8TH Battn Tank Corps. Killed in action 23rd March 1918)*. They used to call me 'Mac' Francis. Anyway, before we drove Tanks they gave us a driving test on lorries. Perhaps I was a bit excited or something, but he failed me for some reason, I was chosen instead to be a Lewis Gunner, I was a good shot you see. When I was training at Bovington, we'd practice with the Lewis Guns by firing at targets in the sand dunes, I suppose they'd be dummy soldiers with the bulls-eye in the middle. I don't know how I got used to it, but after about the first week I was. It was pretty hot in a Tank with the doors closed and always continuous up and down just like a ship at sea. I just seemed to get used to it and it came naturally to me when to fire. I came out pretty good at the end of that. If the driver had been knocked out, the officer on his left would have taken over. If there was nobody else left to take over, they would ask me as I was a second class driver, thank goodness it never came to that! In an emergency, you were interchangeable all

Detail of the Daimler six cylinder, 105hp 'Silent Knight' petrol engine as used in all of the Great War tanks from Mk I to Mk IV

around. The driver and the officer could put the tracks in and change the gears. The starting handle in a Tank was right in the middle and I think two men could have started it if the engine was warm, but usually it took two Lewis Gunners on either side. They were marvellous engines, the Daimler was 105hp and the Ricardo was 150hp,the first Tank I went over the top in had the Daimler. I was positioned right by the side of the engine, it was pretty hot with your back to it. I often doubled up as a gearsman, both in training and in action, if a Lewis Gunner was knocked out the Gearsman could take over. It wasn't only hot inside, it was also very dark. In action if the driver wanted to turn right he would have to put the right track into neutral and the gearsman had to be quick. They would bang on the metal with a spanner, once for first and twice for second. Greasing the Tanks was a terrible job and that would need to be done daily, sometimes if you'd done a lot of travelling, twice a day, but as a rule just once a day. After my training, I didn't get any leave, much to my regret. We went by lorry to Southampton docks. I remember thinking what a bleak place it was, it must have been towards the end of the year and it was very cold. We boarded the troop ship and had a good meal and me and Bernard Gallaher, Barny we called him, went down below as it was so cold on deck. We went down and down and suddenly to our surprise we found at least 100 mules in the hold. We lay down and we slept till morning. It's a wonder we didn't get kicked or killed by these mules, but we didn't and we had a lovely bed for the night in the straw. In the morning some of my other pals asked where we'd been, we'd missed all the excitement. There had been a German submarine chasing us, we had two Destroyers, one on either side. They had dropped some depth charges and we'd lost him. They told us that it had been a rough crossing, the roughest the ship's crew had known. We didn't know anything about any of it down below amongst these mules. We got onto a long French train of cattle trucks, the officers had carriages, there was too much of a contrast. They were in first class saloons and we had 20 men to a cattle truck, they either carried 20 men or six horses. What a slow train it was, every three or four miles we'd stop for a train to pass us or overtake us on a siding. I don't think we ever did more than 10 MPH, more likely it was just walking speed. You could get out and then catch it back up again, we did do, many a time. The Tanks must have come up on flat carriages, about eight to a train. The first Tank would have to drive over seven trucks to get to the top. It was a very tricky job, but I can never remember there being an accident. Mind you, many of them had been chauffeurs in civy life. My pal Gallaher could handle a Tank just like

The Tankodrome or Tank Stables at the Tank Corps Central Workshops in France

a car, he was absolutely marvellous, as was Val Field, he was one of the best drivers in the battalion. We then went on by train to a place called Erin, not the Irish spelling. That was the depot and there was another place where some of the Tanks went, just outside Etaples, I think it was. It must have been cold on this train as we had an empty five gallon drum filled with sand which we'd soaked in petrol. These sand filled drums didn't actually catch fire, I don't know why, but the heat from them was terrific, as was the smoke. When we got out in the morning we were all black, every bit of exposed flesh was completely black from the smoke. Eventually after three or so day's journey we got to this place called Meaulte, we had very nice cosy digs there in a farm. In this farm building, they'd got rid of the cattle and there in the building they had wire netting beds, six beds high up to the ceiling. They were very comfortable indeed, equal to my bed now I think! Anyway, we all slept very well on them and we must have stayed there for about a month. My pal Tuck was a cook, a cockney he was, I used to give him my rum ration. The first time I tasted rum it gave me a headache that lasted for two or three days, it was terrible. I said to myself 'That's the first time I've tasted alcohol and it's the last time!' and I've certainly kept my promise as far as rum was concerned. I used to give the rum to Tuck and he'd give me an egg or two occasionally. I asked him one day where he got them from and he took me to the back of the farm where there must have been 50 hens, maybe more, they were all locked in and covered with wire netting. He'd get up at 5 o'clock before the farmer got up and he'd rigged up a long piece of thick wire about 6 or 8 feet long with a wire scoop on the end of it the same shape as an egg. He'd wriggle this through the wire netting and bring the eggs back with it. He told me that he would take one or two eggs most mornings, just as he fancied them. I'll always remember Tuck for that, he was a rum lad, but a very good soldier. We all got crewed up at Meaulte, Gallaher from Scotland was the driver and Lieutenant Sidebottom from Lancashire was my officer. I was a Lewis Gunner and I forget the other names, we never had a quarrel and we got on very well together. One day the officer said 'Fall in, my crew, I've got to give you a lecture today' It was a nice day, it was cold out, but it was still a very nice day. We went off to this little wood and he said 'Right, make yourselves comfortable, smoke as much as you like'. We all sat around him and he said 'Right, the lecture today is about the Swansea Harbour Improvement Trust'. Do you know what's coming? It was the initials, Swansea Harbour Improvement Trust. He went on to tell us about how when we were taken short we mustn't just do it just anywhere, we must always dig a trench and cover it over afterwards and so on. A week later I had a terrible shock. About a mile or so away from us was a Nunnery and the whole battalion had to form up on parade in this field just outside the Nunnery, we wondered what was going on. The officer eventually told us that it was a Charge Arm or Short Arm inspection! I won't go into the meaning, but there were the Nuns going about their work in the field and they didn't take one bit of notice of what was going on. It really shocked me, you've got the picture in your head haven't you? I won't go into detail. *(The Charge Arm or Short Arm Inspection was a slang term for an intimate examination of the private parts, carried out by the Medical Officer in order to check for infection or injury).* Some of the towns in Northern France had these urinals on the streets which were sometimes only about three feet six inches high, they were for men only. People were passing by on the pavements, shopping and so on and it was very unlike Oswestry! I was just a young bit of grass-seed from the country, I couldn't believe it. When we got back from this inspection we went to look at a model that had been built. They'd brought in a couple of tons of sand and made a landscape on the ground, with little shellholes and little villages and everything. It didn't help us at all when we went over the top. There were no villages left standing when we went over, not one brick attached to another. We did PT and route marches and so on. All this time we were still practicing with the Tank, stripping the Lewis Gun down and so on. We'd practice over and over and that came in very handy later, it probably saved my life. It was fairly stiff at Bovington, but in France, the discipline was very slack. It was relaxed and the food was very good. We had Bully Beef quite often, which I didn't mind and we even had Horse meat once, I didn't like that, it was too tough, but when you're hungry anything will go down. We had the army biscuits, I always liked the army biscuits, but I suppose I had good teeth then, I've got none at all now, only false ones. We used to have Bully Beef stew and I'd get Tucks boiled eggs, we had a very nice time there. This wasn't the Tankodrome, I think that would have been at Etaples or at Erin. I went through the Tankodrome once and there were thousands of them, some all shot up and some being repaired. At Erin I'd never seen so many Chinamen, there must have been thousands of them. They worked very hard, they would do all sorts, even carrying barbed wire up to the line. These were the Chinese Labour Corps. We used to wear overalls in those days, but this stopped after Cambrai, I'll tell you about that later when we get to it. Anyway, one day we all left the depot at Meaulte and the Tanks came on after us on separate trains. We travelled at night about 30 miles or so until we got to a place called Oosthoek Wood, which was in front of Poperinge. We were only about six miles behind the lines and there was a good railway siding there on the right side. It was a very dark night and both sides were firing continuously, they never let up at all. The drivers all got into the first Tank to come out which had also been the first to go on, there must have been a ramp at each end? With care they started to drive forwards down onto the solid ground, I say solid, but it was hardly that. One of my duties was to watch one side of the Tank and the other Lewis gunner would watch the other side as it went along. We'd shout left or right or straight on and the officer was at the front relaying this to the driver by waving his torch in pre-arranged signals. We got to the wood and I was absolutely dog tired. It had been raining for months and months, I found a tree that had been blown over with its roots sticking up it the air. I put my ground-sheet down on the ground and had a pretty cosy time there until we were woken up to camouflage the Tanks. On a specially made double railway truck was an 18inch Naval gun and it had been hit by a Jerry bomb fairly recently and it had been knocked out, useless, I'd never seen a gun like it, tremendously big, a terrible thing really. They built a sand model of the battlefield and shown on it was the road over the Albert Canal and then there was a place called Essex Farm and there was St. Julian and there was a hill and villages. Anyway we went into battle and there was a railway sleeper road that lead from Poperinge to a place called Dirty Bucket Corner. I suppose the Tanks daren't go over it, but some light army vehicles used to use it. We drove along and when we got to the crossroads we had to stop for 19 minutes because every 19 minutes Jerry would put two shells over right onto the crossroads, then he would be quiet for 19 minutes. Every 19 minutes the Military Police on each side would stop everyone and so nobody got hurt there. There were no bodies anywhere on this part of the line, they had cleared them all up, all the men and horses, but the stench was still there. We got past this and then we reached the Royal Albert Canal, there was no water in it and the sides were full of dug-outs. After this we reached our Jumping Off points. There was a barrage going on, but we couldn't hear it inside the Tank. We carried on and we got to no mans land and the stench and the sights became worse. The shelling was terrific and the infantry beat the Tanks hollow. We should have been at the front, but we were right at the back, this was the Third Battle of Ypres. We had orders to go on forwards and the bodies were everywhere, British and German, I'd never seen anything like it and never will. The conditions for the infantry were terrible, not so bad for us unless you got hit. I think I must be the only soldier in the whole of the First World War to say that it wasn't as bad as I'd expected. We must have gone forwards between 500 and 1000 yards. All the shell-holes were full of stinking, dirty, slimy water. There was just mud, not an inch of dry ground anywhere. The debris of war was everywhere, bodies were every-where, British, German, I even saw one or two Portuguese, it was terrible. You never thought for a moment that it would happen to you, I didn't anyway and Field Tommy didn't seem too worried either. There were Mules and Horses, broken guns and the stench was terrible. In the mid-dle of the battlefield we found an old country road, tarmac! We thought, this is grand, but it petered out after about 12 yards and turned into shell holes. We must have covered at least 100 shell holes, but then the last one must have been a big one or the Tank must have been a bit tired. We were going along and suddenly, Zonk! The engine stopped and you could feel the Tank going down and we got the order from the officer 'You two, go and attach the unditching beam' I can't remember the officers name *(E57 Enchantress was commanded by a Lt. Davies)*. We got out of the back door and we got this solid wooden beam fitted to the thick iron chain and then to the track. I was ready to get back into the Tank and I looked across to my pal and he'd fitted his side. We jumped down off the track to get back through the back door when a shell fell within about three yards of me, it must have been a 500lb shell, I'm not exaggerating, I've no need to, it was bad enough without! It never exploded, it just went into the soft ground and made a huge shell hole. I don't know why they were sending the big stuff over because it just went into the ground without exploding, the smaller stuff, 6 pounders and so on, would explode, but the big ones

Made by William Foster and Co Ltd of Lincoln, male Mk II, production number 790, lays stranded in the thick Flanders mud

didn't. It still covered me from head to foot with mud. I got in though the back door of the Tank and I had a terrible headache, concussion. The officer went into the medicine cabinet and got me some stuff, I don't know what it was, but I knocked it back and my headache was gone within about five minutes! Anyway, the Tank wouldn't move, even with the beam on, the ground was just too soft. Our orders were that if we were in trouble, got stuck or knocked out, we should stay with the Tank until 5 o'clock that evening, but it was now only 8 o'clock in the morning. Well, we stayed in this Tank all day and, believe me, the shells dropped all around us, big ones and small ones. The Tank was rocked about, just like a little boat on a rough sea. It went on all day long until about 4 o'clock in the evening when everyone, both sides, got fed up and stopped firing. Our Tank was stuck in a shell-hole only about 150 yards from two German Pill-Boxes, which had been manned that morning, but our infantry had already taken them. I'll never forget all the infantry coming up to support us in amongst the shells that were falling. I didn't see many men fall dead that day, perhaps only two or three. I'll bet no War Correspondent up in his balloon saw more than I saw from inside my Tank that day. Once the time came we left the Tank and went off on foot, me with one of the Lewis Guns over my shoulder and Barny Gallaher with the ammunition. When we got back we were absolutely dead tired, I can't understand why we weren't hit, not one of us was wounded. The stuff was dropping around us, we must have had a guardian angel, I certainly did. We came back past the 12 yards of tarmac road again and it did look lovely, what a picture it was, there wasn't a shell mark on it, it was just like it had been laid the day before. We got over the ridge and past St. Julian and all the other places and suddenly on the side of the road was a bit of a shack. I don't know if it was Red Cross or what, but as we went past someone shouted 'Ere, have a cup of tea!' I told you earlier that I was a tea specialist and that I could buy tea just by looking at it, well I've never tasted anything like this cup of tea in my life, it was absolute heaven, we ended up having two cups each. After that we marched back over the canal and back past Dirty Bucket Corner and when we got back we just fell down asleep in the mud. In the morning we all had lice in our shirts. Even the high officers had lice, no exceptions, everyone serving in France had lice. We used to burn them in petrol, we wasted so much petrol, we'd even swill the mud off the Tanks with petrol every day, not water; we must have wasted thousands of gallons of petrol.

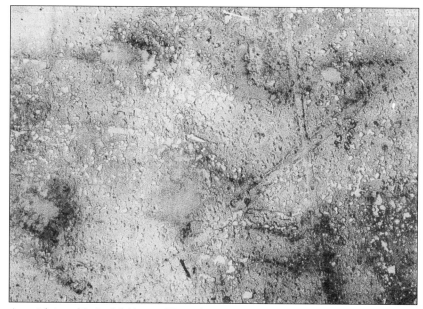

An aerial view of the battlefield around Ypres, the remains of a crossroads can still just about be seen on the left of the picture, but the rest of the landscape is made up of flooded shellholes

The next battle we were in was at Cambrai. We set off and everything was going fine until the Officer of our Tank found that he had lost his bearings, so he said to me 'Get out and see if you can find out where we are. Get in contact with some of our chaps and find out the name of this village on the right here' Jerry had been pushed right back and there were no Germans anywhere, non in sight, except for dead ones. I went back and I was wearing these brownish grey overalls, I also had a revolver on a belt. I went back about 300 yards until I saw a Sergeant leading about 20 or so infantry up a communication trench. I thought that if I carried on and headed for the place where I could see a little building I'd meet him when he came up the lane and I could ask him the name of the village. When I got to about 6 or 10 yards from him he raised his rifle up to me! I shouted 'What the Bloody Hell!' He shouted back at me 'Put your arms up, put your arms up!' I put them up, pretty quick I'll tell you. Anyway, I said 'I'm a Tank, I'm a Tank!' He told me that he thought I was a German officer and that another half a second would have done it, he'd have shot me. It was the nearest I got to getting shot through the heart. I went down to him and the language he turned out, I couldn't repeat, I'd never heard such army language in all my days. He said 'Your people should know better than to dress you like that!' I asked him why he got so excited and he told me that some of his men had been killed yesterday and he was trying to get his first German, to get his own back. Anyway he told me that the village was Graincourt, which wasn't very far from Cambrai. I went back and we got back into the Tank. I think we carried on and it turned out that if that had been Graincourt, we were out of our way a bit and we'd have to turn left a bit to get face on to Bourlon Wood. I could see the fighting going on in Bourlon Wood, it looked like hell, the trees were going up and down from the big Naval gun shells being fired from the back. Don't forget that in a Tank you can't hear the battle, so when the engine stops you get a shock. Anyway we carried on a bit and there was this banging noise. The officer kept on shouting at me 'What's that Francis?' Why he was asking me, I don't know as I was on the right side and the noise was on the left, I shouted back that it was just the exhaust. This noise must have gone on about four times and he kept shouting 'What the hell is that?' and I kept shouting back 'It's only the exhaust sir' I was getting a bit wild with him by now. At last we got it, a direct hit in the left hand side. We got the orders to evacuate the Tank and we all knew exactly what to do. My duty was to carry my Lewis Gun to a place of safety or to a depression in the ground. Gallaher was the driver and his job was to bring the ammunition for the

Not an image that would be immediately associated with the Battle of Cambrai, but after the German counter-attack at least 90 British tanks were captured by the Germans

Lewis Gun. Well, we all got out of this Tank pretty quickly, we were afraid of it going on fire, but it didn't. I remember coming through the grass which was about 12 to 16 inches long and it was lovely dry ground. Anyway, I accidently pulled the trigger on the Lewis Gun and almost accidently shot my pal, it was a very, very near miss. They were firing at us a bit; perhaps it was just one sniper. The officer found a bit of shallow ground, you couldn't call it a trench, more like half a trench. The officer said to me 'Post your gun on the left hand side there Francis, have you got your ammo and everything?' I said that I had and we settled down. Everything was nice and quiet for a good ten minutes and I thought to myself how nice it was, we even had a smoke. We could hear machine gun fire somewhere, but nowhere near us. After ten minutes of peace and quiet a Jerry plane came over us. I could see it coming up from the direction between Bourlon Wood and Graincourt. I had very good eyesight, so I told the officer that there was a Jerry coming up to us. He said 'No it's not, it's one of ours'. I said 'No it's not Sir, it's a Jerry'. He came quite close near to us, I don't know how high he was, but he was fairly low. I could see the Iron Cross on one side, so I put the Lewis Gun up to my shoulder. The officer said 'Put that bloody gun down Francis, it's one of ours'. I knew it was a Jerry, but I had to put the gun down, I had to obey him. Then I remember two Worcestershire Regiment soldiers in front of our little bit and one of them was groaning. Barny Gallaher and I crawled out and got them back, they weren't seriously wounded, one was wounded in the leg and one was hit in the arm, but they were nasty wounds. Soon after, this plane came around again, so I put the Lewis Gun to my shoulder again and of course the officer told me again to put the gun down. By now I'd seen a cross on both sides and I told him, but he still said that it was one of ours. He did wear glasses, he shouldn't have been in the Tank Corps really, his name was Lieutenant Nightingale from Chester, he was an auctioneer, I've been trying to get in touch with his family, but I can't find them. He was one of the finest officers I ever met, there were quite a few good ones, but he was outstanding. He never went to his Dugout without making sure that his crew were cushy for the night, he drank too much Whisky, but he was a fine officer. Anyhow, I put the gun down again for a second time and by Jove if a quarter of an hour later this aeroplane came round again, this time from the left hand side. I put the Lewis Gun up to my shoulder and the officer said 'Put the bloody gun down' and then 'Bloody good shot Francis!' almost as one sentence. As the plane went down I saw the pilot go like this, just gently *(The tape contains no other explanation as to what the pilot actually did)*. Then I did a daft thing, I got up to look whereabouts he was coming down and he was coming down, right near to some Australian Yeomanry who were ready to go over the top with the Cavalry, he came down just by them. About three months after this, we were stationed at Albert and by gum, it was such a cold winter. I went Out of Bounds one day, which was a serious offence in the army, double serious! I had been told that an Australian Canteen down the road had got tinned fruit, hundreds of tins of it, so I thought I'm going to go there. We hadn't had any fruit since we'd been in France and I was dying for a change of diet. I went about six miles out of bounds and got to this Australian Canteen, 'Six tins of fruit please' I didn't even care what kind it was. On the way out I was stopped by the Military Police and they took my name and number. For some reason they didn't confiscate the fruit, he let me take it. When I got back I shared the tins around and we opened them and they were all sweetcorn, we threw most of it away! As I said, it was bitterly cold and when I woke up the next morning I had one boot in bed with me, which was fine, but I'd kicked the other one off and it had frozen, the tongue was like iron and I couldn't get it on. I knew that my name and number had been taken the night before and suddenly the Sergeant Major came round shouting 'Francis, get into the Orderly Room at once!' I knew I was in for the high jump for being out of bounds. Anyway, I shoved this boot on quick and

The actual DFW aeroplane shot down by Gunner Francis photographed a couple of days later on the 23rd November 1917. The Highlanders are searching for souvenirs whilst the man apparently guarding the aircraft seems to be looking the other way (Philippe Gorczynski)

limped over to the Orderly Room. I thought about what I should say, I decided to plead guilty and say that I was dying for some tinned fruit or that I'd got it for my pals and not for me. If I got a chance I'd say that the Officers had all had tinned fruit, but we hadn't. To my amazement the officer and the Colonel got up off the chair and came to meet me as I walked in, they shook my hand! I couldn't make it out. The Colonel said 'Congratulations Francis, you've been recommended for the Distinguished Conduct Medal, but you've been given the Military Medal instead. You're the first one in our Battalion to get the MM in the Battle of Cambrai. Also, the German officer in the aircraft you shot down was the officer commanding he Cambrai area and for some reason he had all of his plans with him in the plane and some very valuable information has fallen into our hands. Thank you, dismissed'.

After the action at Cambrai I told my officer Lt. Nightingale about the incident where I was nearly shot by the infantry Sergeant who thought I was a German. He told me to come with him and tell the Company Officer exactly what had happened. I told him everything and about two months later we got orders through that all Tank crews had to wear their tunic jackets over their boiler suits in future.

Everywhere that a machine gun or a rifle bullet hit a Tank on the outside, the impact would cause a dent on the outside and make a splash of red hot

At a regimental dinner in the 1965 William 'Mac' Francis presents his Military Medal to the 5th Battalion. Accepting it on behalf of the regiment is Colonel Peter Hordern DSO MBE. Colonel Hordern would later become curator of the Tank Museum at Bovington (Ray Hooley)

Colonel Hordern triumphantly holds William Francis's MM aloft.

armour plating on the inside. I got some on my right hand once and it was a hundred times worse than chilblains, it just keeps you awake for two or three nights, but we had to just grin and bear it. We always had the name Enchantress for our Tank. When we got knocked out we drew a new one from Erin and we christened Enchantress II. The name stayed with us all the way through, but I wasn't very enchanted with many of the things I saw, just the opposite. I saw a dirty trick done by our side at the Battle of Cambrai. One of our Sergeants marched about 20 or 30 German prisoners down a communication trench well behind the line. My Tank pal, I don't know his name, but I should have reported him, he shot the lot of them with his Lewis Gun when they were only about 30 yards from him, the Sergeant was leading from the back and could see what he was going to do, so he got down, I was absolutely disgusted.

When Jerry broke through on March 21st 1918 I was at a place called Tincourt Wood and we had about 500 Tanks there. We were there three weeks before and we were told that Jerry was likely to break through at the end of March. It was very boring there, we had no parades and there was nothing to do. I used to go out with my pal from Lancashire and we used to drink Nestles Cafe Au Lait morning, noon and night. It was so slack there, no discipline at all. One day my pal said to me 'The Brigade Headquarters is free this week Mac, anybody from all ranks can go along and have a meal', so off we went. This would have been about a mile or so from Tincourt Wood. We got in there, we had a marvellous meal and we hadn't gone about 200 yards afterwards on our way home when Jerry bombed this place to smithereens! Before that there was a common understanding between the British and the Germans that they wouldn't bomb headquarters; that was the first time that this truce was broken. There was a little iron drain by the side of the lane, it was only about 12 inches square, but I tried to get down it to get away. It was hell, how many were killed or wounded, I couldn't say. It went on for about half an hour and when the barrage stopped, it stopped suddenly, just like that. About a fortnight before the German attack of 21st March 1918 the Colonel got a message from my fathers Doctor at home to say that my father was seriously ill in Oswestry and would the authorities release me for leave. I went up to see the C.O. and he said 'I'm very sorry, but you know what's about to happen, we haven't got long to wait until the Germans attack. I'm sorry that your father is seriously ill, but all leave is stopped, even for officers. Sorry, dismissed'. I saluted him, turned around and marched off, but just as I got to the door he said 'Hold on a moment Francis, just go and wait outside for a moment. I'll just see what I can do, after all you did get the first Military Medal at Cambrai'. After waiting about ten minutes, perhaps a quarter of an hour he called me back in and said 'Leave granted, 19 days in Oswestry, dismissed'. I thanked him very much and of course the German onslaught started on the 21st March whilst I was in Oswestry. I looked at it in the papers and I'll tell you, I was in no hurry to get back, I'm no warrior, I'm a man of peace, all though I might not sound like it sometimes. If I hadn't been given that leave to go to Oswestry I wouldn't be here talking to you today. On my way back I stopped at a French railway station and the RTO, Railway Transport Officer, told me that they had no idea where my battalion was, he said that they knew nothing at all about them. I got sent all over the place and I was two or three days overdue when I finally got back to France. Eventually I found an RTO who told me that he thought my lot were down at Fontainebleau. It was miles away from the front line and the battalion weren't there at all. I was told to go to Amiens, so off I went. By now I was six or seven days overdue, I thought I would be shot at dawn. Luckily I had my Army Book with me, which was stamped every time I passed through anywhere. In the end there were so many stamps in my book that you could hardly make top-nor-tail of it. Anyway, I got to Amiens and had a good meal there. While I was having a meal I met this chap, a signaller, who told me to keep down and watch out as they were collecting everyone together, any rank or regiment and they were sending them up the line to try to stop the Jerry breakthrough. I managed to dodge that, I've never seen anything like it. At about five or six at night I was walking down Amiens High Street and I was wondering what I should do with myself. I wasn't short of money, my father had given me seven golden Sovereigns to take back to France with me, so I was looking after myself all right. Suddenly I heard someone shout 'Francis, where the bloody hell have you been?' It was one of my officers and he had three or four other men with him. 'Where the hell have you been Francis all spick and span, been out with a girl, on the town in Paris?' They were all covered with mud, from top to bottom. I told him that I was overdue and lost and I showed him my Army Book, he took it from me and told me that he would sort it all out and I never heard another word about it. As he finished talking a lorry came down the street with our battalion colours on it. The officer shouted to them 'Any idea where our Battalion is?' and they shouted back that it was just around the corner, so we all got into this lorry and when I got back I found that almost all of my pals, all of my Tank crew, had either been killed or taken prisoner in the German push. This was terrible, I was really disheartened.

The last battle I was in started on 8th August 1918 and that was the one where the British went through for the last time and they just went on and on and on until they got to Germany. We went out on the first day and carried on for about 5 miles. The infantry around us were mainly Australians and New Zealanders, by gum they were marvellous. I would say that by the end of the day we must have gone for more than five or six miles. We got to a little wood and there were Jerry's running from it, one of our Tanks had beaten us to it and suddenly we got a direct hit and it had come from one of our own Tanks! We evacuated the Tank and I saw this German, he came from nowhere and he must have been over 60 years of age. I had my Lewis Gun in my hand and I couldn't fire at him, I just had to let him go. I thought 'I'm not doing my duty', but I just couldn't do it. All the way up the hill we trudged and all the way up a German sniper was firing at us, but he never hit any of us. Seven days afterwards we were due to go over again and I remember the officer saying to me 'Francis, let's get out of the Tank. We're not due to go over for some hours, come and have a smoke with me'. He was Lieutenant Wools, an Australian. We got out and went down into this little dip and he gave me the first cigarette I'd had for about a week and by gum, I was enjoying it. He looked at his watch and said to me 'Two minutes to five, our bombardment starts at five'. Well, this big Naval Gun opened up and I've never heard anything like it, they say that there was one gun to every yard, big ones and small ones. It was the first time I'd heard a barrage, because I'd always been inside the Tank before. Before I could finish my cigarette a shell splinter or one of our own Ack-Ack shells came down by the side of us and ripped the officers leg from top to bottom, I wasn't wounded, or so I thought. Anyway this Red Cross wagon was coming past and I held him up, he said 'Oh, dear, he is in a bad way, get him in the truck and then you jump in too'. I told him that I couldn't, I needed to report what had happened. He kept on telling me to jump into this wagon and I kept on saying no until he eventually told me that it was an order. He was a corporal or a sergeant and so I had to do as he said. When I got in he told me that I'd been hit in the head and I was covered with blood, I hadn't realised. We got down to the dressing station and then onto a train where I met a nurse, but I haven't got time to go into that now. I had got what they used to call a Second Blighty wound, it wasn't bad enough to send you home. I had a nice time there and one day

A contemporary drawing of a huge Railway mounted artillery piece, similar to the type used for the barrage which preceded the Battle of Amiens

I went down to this room for dinner where there were all wounded men, some with arms off, some with legs off, some with head wounds, like me. An officer came in and the Sergeant called for silence. The officer got up onto a big table and said 'Boys, listen to this, the Armistice was signed at 11 o'clock this morning!' Well, I don't think we could take in the significance of it, I certainly couldn't. There was German prisoner of war camp next door and some of the lads rushed out and 5 minutes later each one came back with their arms around the shoulder of a German prisoner of war. They said to the Germans 'Eat, go on eat' and they gave the enemy their own dinner. I was absolutely disgusted with everything, some of the things I'd seen, mangled bodies and so on, but this brought my faith in human nature back to me. It was a wonderful act of human nature.

Official citation for William Francis Military Medal won during the Cambrai operations of the 20th November 1917.

After evacuating the Tank, which had received a direct hit, he joined a small advance party of the infantry and assisted in forming a strong point. When a German two seater aeroplane flew low and fired a machine-gun on the infantry, he retaliated with his Lewis Gun, wounding the pilot and forcing the machine to land. Throughout the whole action he behaved in a most excellent manner and displayed marked coolness.

Lt. John 'Jack' Moss

Aged 93 when interviewed

Notts and Derby Regiment 1914-16
Tank Corps ' F' Battalion 1916-25

When I joined the army I knew little about it and just joined the near-est regiment to me, the Sherwood Foresters. I was amongst miners, mainly redundant or out of work and I found them to be a queer crowd. I went into training on Frensham Common near Aldershot. I went off to France as a Lance Corporal in 1915. We marched immediately up to the line, about a couple of days march and eventually arrived at Armentieres. I saw most of my service within two of three miles of that area. It was virtually stationary in a certain area of the front opposite Armentieres. We used to go back and forth in and out of the line in for a fortnight and then back again to recuperate and have a bath and be cleansed of lice and so on. This went on for month after month until there was sporadic fighting, over the top and up to the barbed wire where they were usually repulsed by the Germans who were very experienced gunners, they were a regular army and we were just children compared with them, do you see. We soon found out that it was very dangerous to put your head out over the top of the trench, never mind about getting out to fight. There was barbed wire and mines and what not in front to stop you, so it was a very difficult situation for the infantry. They thought that mass bombardment would subdue the enemy machine guns. At the first battle of the Somme they'd been firing for a whole week, night and day the sky was bright with the flashes of gunfire. It was continuous, guns going off and shells bursting. They thought they'd absolutely subdued and swamped the German Front Line Trenches and that there would be no opposition from the machine guns. The operation went ahead, minus myself as I'd been sent off down the line. I missed the operation at the Somme by one day. The adjutant came along and said 'Moss, pack your gear and report to the Major who wants someone who can speak French'. I packed up and went down. This saved my life as the battalion went into action the next day and two thirds of them were killed, absolutely massacred on the barbed wire that had not been destroyed by our artillery. The German machine guns were acting as normal because of the deep German trenches. The battle started and

The horror of the trenches was alleviated by camaraderie, friendship and the age old soldiers art of souvenir hunting

out they came and mowed down our people by the thousand. The British command learnt their lesson there. There was sporadic fighting from there on; it became a matter of living as best you could under terrible circumstances. It was low lying land and there was always water at the bottom of the trenches. We had wooden boards at the bottom of the trench called Duck Boards, but very often these would be floating in the trenches and if not they often sank down in the mud when you stood on them.

I did not join the Tank Corps on purpose. As I said, I could speak French and I arrived at Army headquarters where I was being used to interrogate French people coming into the forward area to work, do you see. I had to pass their credentials and say if they were all right. I also had to arrange billets for incoming troops where I used to go around with a Frenchman and we'd take notes of various places where troops, horses and transport could be stationed. This continued for several months until the job ended and they didn't know quite what to do with me, so eventually I was sent down the line to see if I could be any use for interrogation in the forward area. I was then under the command of the APM 8th Army. I served there for a while until Major English said to me 'Your job is coming to an end again, how would you like to go back to England for a commission?' My regiment didn't want me anymore, they'd moved over to Italy, so I was cut off from the Sherwood Foresters. Two of three days later I was back in England on Frensham Common again with the Cadet Corps. After four months training I was commissioned to 2nd Lieutenant and packed off to France to join the Tank Corps. In those days it was actually called the Heavy Machine Gun Corps and before I went off abroad to join the battalion I went to a camp on the south coast for gunnery training, Bovington Camp I think. I already knew Hotchkiss and Lewis guns from my days in the infantry, so I just learnt about the 6 pounders. This lasted just a few weeks and I was soon in the forward area on the battlefield. I joined the 12th Tank Battalion stationed between Albert and Amiens; from there we fought the forward positions and were in and out of action for quite a few weeks. I actually joined them in 1917 and we were in and out of action almost every other day, sometimes these were just an hour there and back. We had to learn how to conserve the Tank, mainly in respect of fuel, the

Mk I tanks of the Heavy Battalion Machine Gun Corps in mid 1916

Tanks would gobble up fuel and you needed to keep a very close eye on that. They had to institute stations in the forward areas so that they could load up and fill up with ammunition and fuel, you soon ran out otherwise. I gained a great deal of experience there in these little actions. It was there that I learned how to drive a Tank properly. The chief function of the officer of a Tank was to negotiate the terrain in which you were fighting, to watch the terrain and give direction to the Tank operatives. It was quite an experience and the actual operations got wider and wider. The main use of the tanks was that the Germans were frightened of them; they'd got no counter to them. They would set up special positions where the Tanks were forced to move into the forward area and cover these areas with artillery fire, which was the only effective deterrent they had to a Tank. This all went on until Cambrai in November 1917, this was the major battle of the Tank Corps and it could not be called a success by any

Mid 1984 and John 'Jack' Moss visits Lincoln to check up on the restoration of Cambrai veteran female Mk IV Flirt II

means. They didn't gain very much territory and had to fall back to the lines not far from where they had first started. In August 1918 the final battle of the war began and this battle was a continuous forward area, the Tanks just kept moving forwards. I think the Germans were on the point of surrendering anyway and the Tanks were just so formidable, they had no counter to them. It is undoubtedly true that the Tank was the final winner of the war. In this final battle I finished up with my two Tanks just outside Mons. This is where we first encountered the Germans in 1914, so actually the war started and finished in the same place and I think this was probably per-arranged. You tried to keep the same crew with you all the time as you knew each other; you were used to each other. An officer would always try to keep the same crew and to know them by name; this seemed to work very well. In 1918 the final battles showed that we'd learnt a great deal and how well the Tanks worked. I could trust them all; the gunners on both sides of the tank would do their own spotting and then shout to me that they could see an object on that side at a certain angle. I would then get the Tanks turned around onto this possible target, do you see. This was all done by pre-arranged signal because of the noise, I could talk to the driver on my right, but that was it. You could have a pee out of the sponson door, but anything more than that would have to wait until you got back. You couldn't feed in a Tank on the move; you couldn't pour tea out as it was lurching about all over the place. You felt safe in a Tank; you never worried about being knocked out. You felt as safe as a house; I never experienced any fear in a Tank, never. I quite enjoyed being in a Tank. The chances of being knocked out were quite remote. We were only in action for a short time; we only had fuel for about an hour and a half, that was all we could carry. I had very little trouble with the Mk IV Tank, you always felt very safe. I never saw any German Tanks, the French had a few Tanks of their own, little light Tanks and I think they did just as much good as ours. A British Tank with a six pounder was all right for a strong point, if you needed to knock something out, but I think the machine gun was the more effective weapon, it can be easily swivelled. A six pounder has one shot and then it has to be reloaded. You would fire, withdraw the shell, reload and so on and by that time you've probably gone passed the thing you wanted to shoot at.

I was sent on a topographical course and became a reconnaissance officer for a while. You were often switched about, they would come around and say that they were short of an officer for this or that and you would need to take over and take this or the other Tank to do a reconnaissance with. I was a little bit above the ordinary as I was very mechanically minded and I spoke both French and German, they made full use of that. As soon as we arrived at the forward area I would go with the forward troops to get the troops billeted. I went with the forward squad to Germany, I crossed Belgium as a reconnaissance officer with the Tanks, it was my job to find our way across and get to our destination just over the Belgian frontier in Germany. I used to go up as recon officer and lay white tapes showing the Tanks where to start an operation. That soon became a job for the Tank commanders themselves. The lines were very near to each other, from

Some of the Ruston Gas Turbine apprentices who restored Flirt II meet 'Jack' Moss who had offered to drive the tank if they got it running again

The history books can only tell you so much, for first hand tips you need someone who was actually there. 'Jack' Moss talks the apprentices through the restoration of one of Flirts machine gun housings

here to the bottom of the garden was a long way! You could hear shells whistling overhead. The Tank battalions were, on the whole, a very happy crowd.

The infantry and the Tanks coordinated very well, the infantry would pick up anyone who surrendered. The Royal Flying Corps also coordinated with us, but I've no idea how they sent massages back. The cooperation was there, but it was all very few and far between. I think that the Tank was the weapon that eventually won the war, without the Tank we never would have won; it shortened the war a great deal.

40074 L/Cpl Ernest Sneath D.C.M.

Age 89 when interviewed

**Motor Machine Gun Corps 1915-16
Tank Corps 'B' Battalion 1916-18**

I originally joined the Motor Machine Gun Corps which was being recruited by the editor of the Autocar magazine. I thought I'd risk trying to get in as I was only 17 at the time and I went to Coventry where I was interviewed by the editor and I got in. We had motorcycles with sidecars with Vickers machine gun mounted on them, but warfare in France became nothing but bogs and trenches and whatever, so motorbikes and sidecars were no good. We were soon transferred to the Heavy Section Machine Gun Corps and we went to Bisley and did our training on Hotchkiss, Vickers and Lewis Machine Guns. After we'd done a great

Men of the Motor Machine Gun Corps equipped with a mixture of Triumph Model H combinations and Douglas 2 ¾ motorcycles

deal of training on guns, including revolver training and rifle training we were moved to a secret area between Thetford and Bury St. Edmunds. The area had been occupied by two battalions of infantry who'd shelled all the farm houses, built craters, machine gun nests, trenches and so on. After we'd been there for a short while and done some more gunnery practice we were introduced to the very first Tanks. At that time we were told that they were water Tanks for the desert. They had no sponsons on them, they were just the bare Tank. They had trailing steering wheels at the back, but these were no good, they just skidded. You could turn on a very slight angle, but if you had a more acute angle you had to lift the tail up using a hydraulic control. The powers that be eventually realized that the tails were no damn good and took them off. You had a hell of a job to turn it at all, even in a slight turn and if you got onto wet ground or skiddy ground they just trailed around, they didn't guide you at all, they were just a nuisance.

We had very extensive training at Thetford and there were two battalions of infantry guarding the area because it was so very secret. If we wanted to go into Bury or Thetford we had to go out with an officer who would give a pass word. We also had to meet the officer again at a certain time in order to get back into the camp with him. After we'd been there a fair amount of time we found that if you brought a few bottles of beer back you could get through the gates all right without the officer being present, this made things a lot easier. We could go out whenever we liked and come back whenever we liked. When we went into town we had to tell people that we were working on Water Tanks for the desert, which seemed to go down pretty well, I think the secret was kept.

After a while we entrained for France and got to the depot over there. We were looking forwards to it, all of us, there was no question of anyone not wanting to go. We had such a good crew and they were all 100% enthusiastic about it, and fortunately so was the officer, he was a grand fellow. We did a certain amount of training in France before we went into action. We trained in some of the trenches, shell holes and so on more or less right at the rear. Our headquarters was quite a distance back at the rear. We did quite a bit of training there, but non under shell fire, although we could hear plenty of it in the distance. Originally I think there were just four companies of us, A, B, C and D, I was in B Company. We were a very happy gang as all of the others had also been recruited by the editor of the Autocar. They came from all over the country, there were some extremely wealthy people amongst us, I wasn't one, but there was one of the Cadburys for instance and one of the Macmillan printing group, there was a very nice chap from Mexico, I'm not sure how he got in. There was another chap who had his own coffee plantations and he got bags of hampers sent to him, he was very generous with them. We were a band of enthusiastic volunteers, I think we'd all gone into this more or less for the adventure, we originally thought we'd all be motorcycling, but this was rather a different thing. We were formed into crews before we went abroad, I had an extremely nice crew, all good members, very enthusiastic. We had a very young officer called Nobby Clark, he wasn't quite as young as I was, but he was still very young. He was one of the Clarks of the Martell Brandy, but we never got sent any brandy. He was quite a decent chap and we all got on very well with him. We were all trained to do all jobs in a Tank; we were all trained on each machine gun, the six pounder, revolvers and rifles. The driver was specially selected and there was only one driver to each crew and I don't think any of the others ever took over with the driving. I was one of those selected to be a driver and I was very pleased to be selected as I'd always been a very keen motorcyclist. Anything with wheels, or tracks in this case, I always thoroughly enjoyed. It was quite different from anything I'd driven before and not easy either.

Once we got going we found the whole area was in a terrible mess, all around Ypres and so on, it was just a complete quagmire. There were dead horses, dead everything in fact all about and we knew we would be going into action. We also knew that it couldn't be a big action, all the powers that be were trying to do at that time was not to advance, but to try to straighten the lines up a bit. The lines around Ypres were in such a mess that it was more or less stuck out on its own with the Germans on both sides. All we were aiming for at first was to straighten the lines. The first Tanks actions were just moral boosters, experiments, I don't think they could have been anything else. I think we only had two companies going for the first actions. I'm not quite sure, but I think there were about

The Cemetery of the tanks. These unfortunate machines are just two of the many that were bogged down or destroyed during the Third Battle of Ypres

82

twelve Tanks to each battalion with three companies to a battalion. The first time we went in we had our infantry all around us cheering like hell, it was such a novelty. Later on they kept as far away from the Tanks as they could! The Tanks attracted the enemy fire and he trained all his machine guns on us and so on, so the infantry kept well away. The first Tanks weren't really armour plated, the armour piercing bullets would go straight through and even the normal bullets would scatter fragments inside a Tank, tiny fragments of red hot boiler plate from the inside plate. Passchendaele Ridge was terrible, an absolute quagmire, it was actually called the Tank Cemetery, because so many Tanks had got stuck. The Germans used land mines and some rolled over land mines and got their tracks broken, but most of them got stuck mainly because the unditching gear was unsuccessful in most cases, the mud was so very deep. We had these unditching beams on the top of the Tanks and fortunately ours worked, we got out and got back, but many didn't. You had to drop it absolutely square; if it dropped at an angle you would soon get stuck. To drop it square, you needed to get both tracks perfectly level with the bolts, which were at certain intervals on each track. You had to fasten the chains on the gear to the tracks, then you needed to lock the differential or one track would skid. Then you would drop it down in front and it would go around. Usually it was the drivers job to fix the unditching beam, you got out of the hatch on top, showing as little of yourself as was possible to the enemy machine gunners, I think we had to use our gear about three times in all, each time in heavy fire. I think we were pretty lucky in our Tank as we got back on most occasions. The first time we went out, a lot of the Germans just ran like hell, they could never have visualized anything like it. It was dawn, it was misty and I suppose it would have been very ghostly to them as we appeared. We got several Germans in the first attack and knocked out several machine gun nests, mainly with our own guns, but once with the Tank itself! We drove straight over it and the Tanks weighed over 30 tons or so. We had a marvellous time in the Cambrai action, it was so well organized. Before Cambrai I'd been out about eight or ten times in action and each time we would return to our headquarters in the wood, if you could call it a wood, there weren't many trees.

At the start of the winter of 1917 we were completely reorganized and quite frankly we didn't like it very much. Our crews were split up to form the nucleus of new Tanks and although the officer and myself stayed together the rest of the new crew were recruited from the infantry. Well, I'm

Female Mk IV tank I 28 Incomparable, lost during the Battle of Cambrai near Bourlon wood on the 24th November 1917. It side-slipped into a trench and although the unditching gear was attached it was not enough to get the unfortunate machine moving again

not sure they were actually recruited; I think they were pushed into it actually, it was all very different. The whole of the regiment's comradeship disappeared, we got on all right with them, but they were all newcomers. They didn't have the same enthusiasm, so we had to do a great deal more training with these new men. I became an instructor and for a while was sent back to the Tank Training Ground near Albert where I was training officers, which I rather enjoyed. We had twenty-two rollers on each track and the rollers needed greasing regularly. The grease gun was just one of those small hand held greasers which you had to turn the screw on. In winter especially it was quite a job, and if I got any superior officers that were a bit snooty, I'd give them that job to do. If I got a good crew who were enjoying themselves, we'd go to a café in Albert and have coffee.

The very first models of Tank we had needed three people to drive them, because the driver only controlled the primary gear and the differential. He needed a gearsman at each side as each track had two gears and a neutral and the only way you could turn was by signalling to the gearsman. If you wanted to turn right you would need to signal to the gearsman on the right to get into neutral while the gearsman on the left got into either first or second gear. Originally you would signal to the gearsman by banging on the bonnet *(engine casing)* on the respective side, but on occasion due to the noise a gearsman on the wrong side also heard the signal and you found yourself in neutral on both sides. Sometimes you'd find that the chap on the right hand side was in first gear while the man on the left hand side was in second and then you had a bit of a twist up, it was a bit complicated. Apart from the noise, on many occasions it was so hot and

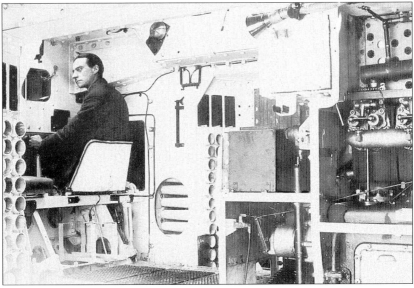

The deceptively clean and empty looking interior of a brand new tank, fresh from the production line in England. In reality this machine would be filled with ammunition, eight men, petrol vapour exhaust smoke and cordite fumes (Tank Museum Bovington)

fume filled inside a Tank that everyone was very sleepy, do you see? After a while they installed sets of lights which the driver operated to indicate whatever gear he wanted on whichever side. These were completely useless as if the chap was looking at them permanently he was more of less memorized and he was already half asleep with the heat, so he would usually end up ignoring the lights and eventually we went back to banging on the bonnet. We had six Gunners in a Tank and an Officer and a Driver at the front, making up the crew of eight. Two of the gunners would double up and be the gearsmen. We had a female Tank which had Lewis Guns, two in each sponson and the driver and officer had another between them in the central ball and either of them could use it. We all had revolvers, because a rifle was no good inside a Tank. The main problem with the original Tanks was the Daimler Sleeve Valve engines. They had very thick oil, not modern, thin oils like we have today, so it took four men to start the engine. Between the engine and the gearbox was a platform and above that the starting handle went in between the two. You had two men on each side winding the starting handle over and you can take it from me that it was quite a job! The Driver in the original Tank had a small crank magneto which he wound like blazes in the hope that it would give a better spark, so there was a great deal of relief when the engine started. When we changed from the Daimler to the Ricardo engines, things became much better. The Ricardo was a good engine, it wasn't sleeve valve and was more powerful and the starting was a tremendous amount easier, but it still wasn't perfect.

By mid 1917 the powers that be were beginning to realize that all of the recent actions had been terribly expensive in both men and materials and had resulted only in a slight straightening of the trench. We started to hear many rumours that there was to be a large offensive to break though. In the mean time the Germans had built the Hindenburg Line, which was supposed to be absolutely Tank proof. It was so wide and so deep that when a Tanks nose got down into it, it would be stuck for good. We were moved back to a special area which had a reconstruction of a section of the Hindenburg Line built in it for us to experiment on. For this purpose we had fascines which were brushwood to a diameter of some eight feet and extended to the width of both tracks. It was bound with chains and it was carried on top of the undiching rails. When we dropped it into our section of the Hindenburg Line we could get across and out quite successfully as the tail of the Tank rested on the brushwood fascine. Eventually we moved up to the front, complete with our fascines and undiching beams, and it was really remarkable as we managed to get the Tanks into no mans land before dawn without the Germans knowing. We did this by following white tapes that had been laid out on the ground over our line and into no mans land. In addition to the tapes an officer would walk in front of the Tank holding a lighted cigarette which he would hold behind him for us to follow, it was a very hazardous job. We had to keep the Tank engine just ticking over, we daren't accelerate. Even if we went into a shell hole we couldn't accelerate, we had to come out with it just ticking over. We would be lucky to be doing one mile per hour. Occasionally we'd lose the officer in a shell hole or something and have to stop until we found each other again. It was the only occasion on which we went into action without a barrage. We'd had no previous barrage at all, it was simply a case of trying to take the enemy by surprise, that way, when zero hour came, all hell was let loose. Every gun we had opened up, it was absolutely fantastic. We started off and eventually got to the Hindenburg Line. We managed to drop our brushwood; it was very difficult to drop it dead straight. If you didn't drop it dead straight it would fall on a slant and you'd never get out. We dropped ours straight and we got over with no difficulty, it clawed a bit on the far bank as it was very high, but we got over all right. Once over we had a fantastic time, we were way ahead of the infantry and the Germans ran like we'd never seen before and we got into country where there was still trees and houses. One of our objectives was Marcoines where there was both a railway and a canal, also there was a road. We had to make sure there were no mines. We got to our objectives and did a check for mines and then carried on further ahead. We got to a village where there wasn't a pane of glass broken. We disturbed the Germans at breakfast; they were having ham and eggs. There were chickens running about, it was quite unseen in trench warfare. One of the gunners and myself got out of the Tank as there was no sign of any Germans. We went into a Château, with our revolvers out. Suddenly we heard movement in one section of the building and we kicked the doors open expecting to find Germans, but instead we found two German horses. We thought, lovely, we'll take these back with us. We mounted up and just at that moment the Germans opened up with high explosives all around us. We set off as fast as we could and unfortunately I seemed to have picked the servants horse, as it wouldn't move except with its nose up the backside of the other one. Anyway, we managed to get them back to where we were billeted in some small cottages. We had visions of selling these horses on and making a bit of money. During the evening a Cavalry officer and his servant came up to me and asked about the horses and said 'I'm commandeering them, I've lost mine and so has my servant'. He took his hip flask out and had a swig, offered one to his servant, but not to us. We didn't even get a drink in return for our horses. The next morning we could have carried on further, but we had no infantry support, so we had to come back to where we'd started. A few days afterwards the Germans put up a very stiff counter offensive. We were at a little village called Gouzecourt where we were trying to make good Tanks out of bad ones. So many had been hit that we were swapping the sponsons and so on. One of the other companies were sent out and we went with them in

The sight of an unspoiled village would have been a great surprise to Ernest Sneath, this photograph shows the devastation that was once the village of Flers in mid 1917 and is more typical of what Mr. Sneath would have been used to

what Tanks we had and we managed between us, to hold the Germans back. It was a funny feeling to see everyone else coming back, even the Guards! We got to this place and there was a ration train there which had been shelled and stopped. Two of us got out and had a look round, we got cases of cocoa au lait, coffee au lait and a cask of rum! We went back and got them into the Tank, the officer was very sporting about it and we were very popular with the others upon our return as they all soon heard about this cask of rum we had.

I think the most miserable time we had was during the winter of '17, which was the worst winter we'd had, it was terrible and everything was frozen solid. It was so bad that we had to go out and start the engines every hour, we had no anti-freeze, I don't even think it had even been invented. Then when the thaw set in, it was utterly impossible to move anything for at least a month, because the thaw was so deep that everything was absolutely stuck in the thick mud.

After Cambrai we had various actions and the front was more or less stabilized after the German counter-attack in 1918. They had got quite a bit of their land back and soon we were sent in again to try to regain this lost land. It was August 1918 and we were going into places that were supposed to be occupied by the Germans and they weren't, they had retreated miles, it was the beginning of the end for them. Unfortunately, during this action our Tank caught a high explosive straight through the top and we got out as best we could in the middle of a very heavy German barrage. The officer and myself made for a shell crater and found shelter there whist the shells were falling all around. We decided to make a run for it, we were both wounded, although not too badly. It was all such chaos that we were not quite sure which way to go, anyhow we decided on a direction. Fortunately it was the right direction as we stumbled into a trench and it was full of British soldiers. We were both sent straight off to a casualty clearing station and I'm afraid that was the end of my active service. I'm fairly sure that the rest of the crew all got out of the Tank all right, but they headed off in the other direction and found a shell-hole there. Although we tried to trace them afterwards we were unable to find any trace of them. I think all of the records were so topsy turvey.

I went off to this CCS and after hospital I was sent to an American convalescent camp at Trouville. I had a marvellous time there, the Americans were really wonderful. I had all the Dollars I wanted and as much food as I could eat, it was wonderful. Once I had fully recovered I was due to go back to our base, but all along the way every time the train stopped at a station French people would come and ask if we knew anything more about the war being over. There were rumours everywhere that it was all over. Me and this other Tank man who was also on the train finally got to our base and we wandered up to our headquarters. Just as we got there everyone was out parading on the parade ground and it was there, just as we arrived, that it was officially announced that the war was finally over, peace had been declared. The whole of the unit ran down to Le Trapour and drank the place dry, I was too damn tired so I went into camp instead. After peace had been declared I got fourteen days leave and went off home. I was given a medal, just for general service I think. You see I was lucky enough that on every occasion except for our last action I brought my Tank back, which quite a lot didn't. Whilst still on leave, through various telegrams and so on I was told to report to Rippon for discharge and so I never went back to my unit and that was the end of my war.

Official citation for Ernest Sneaths Distinguished Conduct Medal.

For conspicuous gallantry and skill as first driver of a Tank during operations extending from March to September 16 1918.

Near Beugny, on March 22 1918, he displayed exceptional courage and coolness in action, which inspired his crew with confidence.

During the August 1918 operations, near Villers-Bretonneux, he set a splendid example of gallantry and devotion to duty, his skill and initiative being very marked. During the period he has on three occasions reached his objective and has proved himself to be a determined and resourceful driver. His conduct throughout all engagements is deserving of the highest praise.

490930 2nd/Lt.
George Edward 'Ted' Waddington

Aged 89 when interviewed

13th London Regiment 1914-17
Tank Corps 'H' Battalion 1917-18

When I was 17 I got a job in Barclays bank in Wisbech. In 1914 when war was declared I asked the manager if I could join the army as all my friends were already in the Yeomanry, but he said no. Another month passed and I asked again and he said no, I asked him again in November and again he said no. The other fellows in the bank said 'You only keep asking because you're scared to go, you know he's going to keep on saying no' I said to them 'If it's a fine day, I shall play football, if it rains I'll join the army' That was a half day, so we had the afternoon off from work and damn me if at 1 o'clock it started to rain. I got the next train to London and got out at Liverpool Street station where I saw this fellow in khaki. I asked him where I could join the army and he asked me what regiment I wanted to join, well I didn't know one regiment from the other. He says to me 'I'm just going back to the 13th London's in Kensington, come with me'. He must have realized I wasn't a Londoner. By the time we got there it was getting on for 6 o'clock and they'd finished recruiting, so I said 'what do I do now'. He told me that they started recruiting again at 9 am the next morning and I could stay there and sleep in the barracks. I went across to the Holland Arms and got some food there and afterwards went back over to the barracks thinking I was going to sleep there, of course I didn't have any sleeping clothes at all. I stopped at the barracks for about half an hour and they all seemed to be more drunk than sober. I thought, 'I'm not used to this I'll go back over to the Holland Arms'. I did just that and I spent the night there.

Next morning we paraded at 9 am and I joined up, that was the Thursday. We paraded again later and we were told that was that and we were dismissed until Saturday morning. I went to the office and told them 'That's all very well, but it's no good to me I live in Soham'. He said 'Get half fare back and go home until then'. That's just what I did; I got half fare back and went off home. When I saw my father he said 'now what have you done?' I said 'I've joined the army'. He said 'I know, I've had a wire from your manager telling me that you've left the bank'. He asked me what I'd joined, but I'd got no idea, I knew it was a London regiment. He told me that I should send a wire to my manager at the bank and let him know what had happened. Instead I sent a wire off to this girl I knew and I signed it Ted. She got this wire from Ted and said to herself 'I don't know anyone called Ted' she asked her sister and her father, but neither of them knew Ted either. Her father said that she should go and meet me and so she did. We spent a very pleasant night at the pictures and so on and I never did get in touch with the bank.

I got back to London on the Friday night by the mail train, I can't remember where I slept, and then I went off to the barracks on Saturday morning and blow me if they didn't say dismissed again until Monday! I talked to one of the lads and told him about the drunkenness at the barracks and how a didn't really want to stay there and he told me that he was staying at a boarding house in Westbourne Grove. The landlady had two daughters and we used to take them out and thoroughly enjoyed ourselves. Once the new year arrived we marched from there to Saffron Walden where we all ended up catching ground colic. Every time we went out marching or on parade, half of us were ducking out to go behind the hedges. At the end of May I joined a draught of around 50 men to go out to France, Saint Omer as it turned out. We went up to the line at the beginning of May and on the 9th of May we went over the top at the Battle of Festubert. We got cut to pieces at that battle. We were then sent to relieve the London Scottish who'd got themselves into a bit of trouble, well we ended up in about as much trouble as they were. Just 39 of us answered roll call the next morning, I think that was about May 10th. We came back down to a village just outside Saint Omer. Soon we formed the regiment back up again and we were back in the line, in and out, in and out until we ended up at Gommecourt for an attack on 1st July 1916. We dug all these trenches to practice going over the top. In the real thing we got cut to pieces going over the top. Coming up through the village we could see the Germans marching up the road about four deep and there were a lot of them. We thought that the best thing to do was to get back to our own lines. We threw away our rifles and took our equipment off and ran like hell, it must have been about 800 yards. Only about two or three of us got back, where we picked up some other peoples equipment and rejoined the line. We carried on as

The remains of the village of Festubert in mid 1915, much as it would have been when Ted Waddington first saw it

A Vickers machine gun team in action wearing their early Gas Hoods

before, in and out of the line, we had no end of new replacements. Eventually, somewhere near Arras I went over the top and the machine guns were barking away and I was in a hurry to get down out of the way. I fell into this trench and there was a blinking German sat there with a bayonet on his rifle and he stuck it in my bleeding leg, I shot him. I hobbled down to the dressing station to see the Doctor. He washed my leg, put iodine on it and bandaged it and said report back to your battalion. I was very disappointed, I thought I'd got a Blighty one, but it wasn't. Soon I began to think, this is no use I can't last much longer, I've been out here for 18 months, so I applied for a commission. This was just before the Battle of Arras started and our Colonel said that he wouldn't let anybody go until the battle was over. I came through it all right again and eventually got back to England.

I applied for a commission in the Tank Corps because I thought it took longer to train you up there than anywhere else. Anyway this officer asked me why I wanted to be in the Tanks and I told him that I was interested in machinery and that I'd had a motorbike before the war and he said 'Splendid, as long as you're interested in machinery' and signed my papers. I went off to Perbright, I think it was, for training and had a very fine time. The first time that you get into a Tank you are rather surprised by the amount of things already inside. There were two seats at the front, one for the driver on the right and one for the officer, where I sat, on the left. You had two other men at the back. As you drive forwards there is

The ability to ride a motorcycle and a passing knowledge of how the internal combustion engine worked would have made any of these five Despatch Riders prime candidates for the Tank Corps

a hell of a noise, you can't hear anything and you're only doing about 4 miles per hour. If you wanted to turn you had to bang on the tin engine casing to attract the attention of one of the other chaps who would change gear. Then you had a 6 pounder gun on either side with machine guns behind. This Colonel came over to us from the infantry and one day he thought he'd like to go for a ride in a Tank. He said 'Well, you're not going very fast' and I told him that we could only do 4 miles per hour. He said 'That's no good; you'll have to go faster than that when you get to France'. He wouldn't believe that we could only go at this speed. He said to me 'Can't you go any faster downhill' and I told him that we could, but only if we put it in neutral and let it roll. He told me that I should do just that. We ended up sheering the brake band trying to stop it and there was a hell of a row about it. I was Court Marshalled where I had to tell them that the Colonel had ordered me to do it and that I was only obeying orders, so they got the Colonel in and he told them that he'd ordered me to do it and they had to let me off, he got a ticking off and that was the end of that.

We had the same crew all the time whilst we were training, I think the battalion went off in 1917, but after some months training I was playing football and broke my collarbone. This happened just as the battalion were ready to go off to France and I was left at home as Orderly Officer for several weeks. This Army order soon came through saying that anyone who'd been in the depot for more than 3 months would be transferred to the infantry. Me and my pal Smith decided it was too dangerous in the infantry and a damn sight less dangerous in the Tanks so we put our names down to go to France. They soon found out that I'd been an NCO in the infantry and said we could do with a drill instructor here, so I thought that suits me very well and I got the job of Drill Instructor. Old Smith says to me if you're not going into the line then neither am I. He had a gammy knee and used to sit there and knock it about until it swelled up so much that he couldn't get his trouser leg over it. This stopped him going up the line and they gave him the job of Orderly Officer. We stayed there for a while until I was sent up to join the forth battalion. I went over the top in a Tank with them no more than once or twice before the Armistice was declared. During the armistice we had a very nice time. We used to just parade once in the morning, we were billeted in a nice little farm-house and the mess was in the local pub. I was quite an athlete and won several prizes in the Tank Corps sports days. I was going to represent the Tank Corps in the hurdles at a competition in France when my demobiliza-

A very dashing young Edward Waddington, newly commissioned and transferred into the Tank Corps (Ray Hooley)

tion papers came through. I decided that I'd been away from England for rather a long time and I'd much rather home, thank you very much.

Once I got home I had nothing to do, there were no jobs about and eventually I thought the best thing I can do is go back to the bank, so I went off back to Wisbech. When I got there, the very stern faced local director was there. I asked him if I could have a job, I used to work here and I've been off in the army. He said to me 'Yes, I know you, your name is Waddington. You set a very bad example to the rest of the staff when you were here before by leaving without giving proper notice. I will not recommend you for a job with the bank'. I went off home again. Shortly afterwards I got a letter from my old manager who was now Manager at the Peterborough branch. I went off to see him and he offered me a job at £120 per year plus a bonus of 10%. When I'd been a specialist full Lieutenant overseas in the Tank Corps I'd been getting £600! In the end I had no choice and I took the job at the bank in Peterborough.

Acknowledgements and recommended reading

Anon.   1945   A Short History of the Royal Tank Corps
                             Gale and Polden LTD, Aldershot

Anon.   2007   Mechanical Maintenance of the Mark IV Tank
                             Friends of the Lincoln Tank, Lincoln

Baccarne R.   2007   Poelcapelle 1917. A Trail of Wrecked Tanks
                             Privately Published in Belgium

Bader P &   1998   More Local Heroes
Hart-Davis A.   Sutton Publishing LTD, Worcester

Beddows K.   1999   Metro-Cammell, 150 years of Craftsmanship
C & S Wheeler   K Beddows, C Wheeler, S Wheeler and
                             Runpast Publishing

Boin W.R.   1997   War Memoirs 1917-19
                             H. Karnac Books Ltd, London

Breyette T.W.   2000   Tank Killers, History of the Tank Destruction
Bender R.J.   Badge
                             R. James Bender Publishing, California

Campbell C.   2007   Band of Brigands-The First Men in Tanks
                             Harper Press

Clark R.H.   1998   Steam Engine Builders of Lincolnshire
                             Society for Lincolnshire History and
                             Archaeology

Cooper B.   1974   Tank Battles of World War I
                             Ian Allan Ltd, Shepperton

Fletcher D.   1984   Landships. British Tanks of the first
                             World War - HMSO, London

Fletcher D.   1991   Mechanised Force, British Tanks Between
                             the Wars - HMSO, London

Fletcher D.   1994   Tanks and Trenches
                             Sutton Publishing, Stroud

Fletcher D.   2001   The British Tanks 1915-19
                             Crowood Press, Ramsbury, Marlborough

Forty G. & A.   1988   Bovington Tanks
                             Dorset Publishing Company, Sherborne,
                             Dorset

Forty G.   1989   Royal Tank Regiment,
                             A Pictorial History
                             Guild Publishers

William Foster   1920   The Tank. Its birth and development
and Co LTD   Bemrose and Sons, Derby and London

Gibot J.L.   1999   Following the Tanks, Cambrai
Gorczynski P.   Imprimerie Centrale de l'Artois, Arras

Glanfield J.   2001   The Devils Chariots
                             Sutton Publishing, Stroud

Guderian H.   1999   Achtung Panzer!
                             Brockhampton Press

Hickey D.E.   1936   Rolling into Action
                             Hutchinson, London

Lane M.R.   1997   The Story of the Wellington Foundry,
                             Lincoln - Unicorn Press, London

Liddell Hart B.H. 1934 The History of the World War 1914-1918
Faber and Faber LTD, London

Liddell Hart B.H. 1959 The Tanks. The history of the Royal
Tank Regiment
Volumes I and II
Cassell and Co LTD, London

The Lincoln Tank 1988 Tank Papers
Group Moorprint, Lincoln

Macksey K. 1988 Tank versus Tank
Guild Publishing

Mills D. (Editor) 1989 History of Lincolnshire Volume XII;
Twentieth Century Lincolnshire
The History of Lincolnshire Committee,
Lincoln

Mitchell F. 1933 Tank Warfare
Thomas Nelson & Sons Ltd, London

Moore W. 1988 A wood called Bourlon-The Cover up
after Cambrai
Leo Cooper Ltd, London

Parker C. & 2000 Aircraft Made in Lincoln
Walls J. Society for Lincolnshire History and
Archaeology

Parker T. 1995 The Tanks at Flers. Volumes I and II
Fairmile Books, Surrey

Peglar M. 1982 The Tank Corps. Honours and Awards
1916-1919
Midland Medals, Birmingham.

Pullen R. 2007 The Landships of Lincoln-Second Edition
Tucann Print and Press

Reynolds J.   1999   Engines and Enterprise,
                                 The Life and Work of Sir Harry Ricardo
                                 Sutton Publishing, Stroud

Rigby W.   1923   The evolution of the Tank
                                 Unpublished Article held by
                                 Lincoln City Archives

Ruston and   1920   Our Part in the Great War
Hornsby Ltd   Bemrose and Sons, Derby and London

Schneider W &   1990   German Tanks in World War I. The A7V and
Strasheim R   Early Tank and development
                                 Schiffer Publishing, Pennsylvania

Smithers A.J.   1986   A New Excalibur
                                 Book Club Associates

Stern A.   1919   Tanks 1914-1918, The Logbook of a Pioneer
                                 Richard Clay and Sons, London

Swinton E.D.   1932   Eyewitness
                                 Hodder and Stoughton Limited, London

Van Emden. R   2005   Britain's last Tommies
                                 Pen and Sword Military, Barnsley

White B.T.   1978   British Tank Markings and Names
                                 Squadron/Signal Publications, Michigan

Whitmore M.   1989   Mephisto. A7V Sturmpanzerwagen 506
                                 Queensland Museum, Brisbane, Australia

Williams-Ellis C.   2007   The Tank Corps
Williams-Ellis A.   (Originally Published 1919)
                                 The Naval and Military Press

Wilson A.G.   1986   Walter Wilson: Portrait of an Engineer
                                 Gerald Duckworth and Co Ltd, London

Wright P.   2000   Tank, the progress of a monstrous war
                            machine - Faber and Faber, London

This book would not have been possible without the kind assistance of the world renowned industrial historian, Ray Hooley, who owns all copyrights and permissions to the original taped recordings from which the majority of the text is taken.

Unless otherwise stated, the photographs and illustrations used in this book are from the authors own collection.

The views expressed by the six veterans in this book do not necessarily reflect the views of either the author/editor or the publishers.